MW01592376

CONTENTS

INTRODUCTION

Congratulations on purchasing *Empath,* and thank you for doing so.

The human connection is a remarkable ability. *What makes us connect and disconnect from the people around us?* Why do we feel so strongly about some relationships than we do about others? We may be different and unique individuals, but there are three things we all share in common: *We want to be seen. We want to be understood. We want to be heard.* That is the essence of empathy and what it means to be an empath. Now, most people understand empathy, but they're not quite sure what it means to be an empath. Even some empaths might not fully understand the gifts they possess.

What is an empath anyway? Well, an empath is simply an individual with a high ability to be able to hear information, gather it, assimilate it, and use this knowledge to understand the people around them better than most people can. An empath is an individual who is so sensitive to their surroundings that they are able to not only listen with their ears, but they can also feel the exact emotions someone might be experiencing, read body language, and absorb everything a person is telling them. Some empaths can understand a person better than that person understands themselves. They are highly-sensitive individuals, and if someone around them is displaying really intense energy, the empaths feel that energy but at a magnified level. For example, if someone was feeling sad, the empath would feel that sadness 10 times more. The emotional situation of others registers at a very high level for the empath.

If you've ever been told, *"You're very sensitive,"* you might have the qualities of an empath. If you feel the emotional pains of others so strongly, you might be an empath. Emotions are a part of who we are, and while everyone experiences emotions, empaths experience it on an entirely different level. The ability to be able to walk in someone else's shoes, to see things from their perspective and experience everything that they are feeling is a unique gift. If you're an empath in today's digital world, you possess a gift that is so rare and so overlooked that it is easily forgotten. Most people today are so consumed with what's going on in their own lives and what's happening in the online world that they have lost touch with the ability to connect on a human level. Yes, being an empath is a gift, but if you don't know how to manage this gift, it can quickly become a weight that feels like it's too much to bear.

By the time you get to the end of this book, you're going to have the tools and information you need to help you better manage your empathic abilities and restore balance in your life.

There are plenty of books on this subject on the market, thanks again for choosing this one! Every effort was made to ensure it is full of as much useful information as possible; please enjoy!

THE EMPATH IN ME

WHAT DO WE MEAN BY "EMPATHY" or "compassion"? What makes us care about someone else's feelings? How do we even tell what they are feeling in the first place? Imagine walking down the street, and you come across a homeless person. You feel bad, even sorry for them partially stemming from your personal distress at the situation and nothing to do with their emotional state. Maybe you give them some money to take away some of the guilt you feel. In this scenario, one of two things can happen. If you're too focused on alleviating your own distress, you'll simply avoid the uncomfortable situation and not try to grasp the other person's mental state and how they must be feeling. In contrast, when you focus on their emotions, you're able to act altruistically and genuinely feel for them. The sympathy and compassion you feel don't necessarily mean you feel exactly what they are going through, but rather you feel *alongside* what they may be experiencing.

Suppose you want to find out exactly how someone else is feeling.

How would you go about it? One approach would be to ask them directly how they feel, but then again, people can always hide their feelings. Sometimes they might not even understand how they truly feel in the first place and find it difficult to explain. The other approach is the logical approach. When you see someone smiling, you can deduce that they must be feeling happy, hence the reason for the smile. Then there is the other approach of putting yourself in the person's shoes, by imagining how you would feel if you were homeless. That's empathy.

Introduction to Empathy

Empathy. It is a word you've probably heard several times in your life, enough to get a general understanding of what it means. But the only way to truly understand empathy and what it means to be an empath is to *experience it.* This refers to the ability to recognize the emotions in others. *How does someone else feel in a situation? How do they respond to someone or something?* This is a skill that is going to take you far, especially professionally, because like self-awareness, having empathy is the key to helping you decipher the way someone else feels. This, in turn, will help you decide how you should respond and manage the situation. It will help you determine the best approach to use with them. Having empathy will help you anticipate the needs of another because you recognize the emotions that they are displaying. It helps you develop understanding and enhances your social skills. It is the tool that you need to help you develop good interpersonal skills, and effectively become an agent of change. It helps you become a better leader, communicate better, and even be able to exercise influential power over the people that you need to manage. It is the tool that is going to help you build and nurture meaningful bonds.

There's a difference between sympathy and empathy too, which is important to acknowledge before we dive deeper into the subject. *Sympathy* acknowledges someone's pain or difficulty. Sympathy might sound something like this:

"I'm so sorry this is happening to you."

"I can't believe that happened! I'm sorry to hear that."

"That must be really tough for you; I'm so sorry you're going through it."

Sympathy acknowledges that what the other person is going through is difficult and hard, and you are affected by that because you feel genuinely sorry they're going through a rough time. *Empathy*, however, takes it a step further. Empathy goes beyond the logical mind. It goes beyond the thinking and beyond the rational part of the mind too. Empathy envelopes the emotion and the state of being that the other person is in, and connects with them on their level. A lot of the time, empathy could be displayed without having to say much. There could be no explanation or the desire to "fix" the problem. Empathy creates a sense of "oneness" with the person you're experiencing it with. For example, let's say you just got the news that a very good friend of yours is diagnosed with a serious health problem. Your friend had this seemingly perfect life and everything going for them. All of a sudden, life hits the brakes, and their whole world is turned upside down by this news. Empathy allows you to feel exactly what they are going through. The shock at receiving such news, the questions that linger about where do you go from here, and probably every single emotion they must be experiencing. You find yourself crying, bawling your eyes out the way your friend must have done when they first got the news because you cannot believe this is happening. You experience all the same overwhelming emotions your friend did. You're in a state of grief and pain, just like they are.

Empathy can bring a real sense of comfort. Often, people who are going through a hard time need you to "be" with them, and this does not always mean help them fix a problem. There's a sense of comfort that comes from knowing someone completely and whole-heartedly understands what you are going through. When you find yourself in those moments where you don't always know what to say or how to act, pause for a minute. There is no "right way" to approach every emotional situation, and that is the beauty of empathy. It allows you to show your support by *being there* for them. Be the refuge that the other person needs.

Empathy is a necessity because life is built on relationships. Relationships are what life is all about. We've got a relationship with our families, friends, colleagues, partners, spouses, and various other people we may meet as we journey through life. Some relationships mean everything to us, and obviously, we would want to do everything that we can to keep the relationship healthy. Once a relationship has been damaged, it can often be hard to piece back together; sometimes, it can't be fixed at all. This is why empathy matters, because it provides you with the knowledge, tools, and skills that you need to foster and nurture these relationships, to keep them healthy and always thriving. Empathy helps you relate to the people closest to you and the people around you. It helps you to understand how you should react and respond to situations in the best possible manner. It helps you form deeper, more mean-ingful bonds because you can understand what the people around you may be feeling and see things from their perspective. The ability to empathize is going to benefit you in so many ways. It helps you resolve conflicts better and manage disagreements when you can empathize with others. It helps you accurately predict how others are going to react. It makes you more confident at expressing your point of view because you're attuned to your surroundings.

When you're attuned to the emotions and feelings of other people, they will view you as a source of comfort, sometimes even as someone you can heal them emotionally. It improves your motivation to become better and the ability to thrive in any social setting. You form better and stronger bonds with the relationships that you forge, even the new one. You will find it much easier to forgive others because you can see things from their perspective, reflect on why they reacted that way, and understand where you're coming from. It makes you more aware of your non-verbal body language and the way you come off to others. If you want to wield any kind of influence, you need to have empathy on your side. When you fail to sense the way that others around you feel, your social interactions will suffer as a result. You will find it very difficult to build effective rapports, and even to form solid bonds. People must be able to like you, trust you, and relate to you if they are going to allow themselves to be influenced by you.

Signs You Might Be an Empath

What springs to mind when you think of the word empath? Do you believe that empaths are people who have already been born with that gift? That's a common misconception, although true in some cases. But being an empath is a skill that you can learn. Becoming an empath is about training your mind, exercising it to become more attuned to empathy. It is about shifting your mind-set, training it until empathy becomes second nature to you. It further enhances your ability to relate and understand those around you. Someone who is a skilled empath is someone who is effective at reading emotional cues. They are able to listen effectively to the voices of the people around them because they have a genuine understanding of where that person is coming from.

Empaths are compelled to help others because they are able to grasp the experience of another in a way not many people can. Abigail Marsh, a neuroscientist, and psychologist, wrote a book in 2017 called *The Fear Factor* in which she describes the evidence she has found. Marsh explains that there is a difference between the brains of people who are highly empathetic compared to everyone else. She refers to these groups of individuals as *altruists*. Empathy is no doubt a valuable skillset to have. It leads to stronger and more trusting connections with the people around you. It helps you figure out how to act appropriately in social situations. However, being an empath can also be a very draining experience. The intensity of the emotions that are felt by empaths is so powerful it can often leave them feeling drained as though they went through the emotional experience themselves, that is how vividly they experience these emotions. Being flooded with emotions is a difficult thing to go through, and it can negatively impact your mental health if you don't do something to take care of yourself. This is even more significant when the emotions you experience aren't yours.

Being an empath is not just a skill for someone who was born with that natural gift. It is something we all can learn. Empathy is not just about working on controlling and understanding emotions; it is about learning to act, be and care. These should slowly start to become part of your personality. By simply changing your attitude, displaying a little love and care, you would be surprised at what a world of difference it can make. With their highly sensitive nature, empaths are likely to feel overwhelmed by crowds and loud noises. They are also prone to feeling completely exhausted to the point of fatigue. Awareness is where it all begins, and it is important to know if you and empath before you can take the necessary steps needed to bring balance to the experience. Here are the signs you might be an empath:

- **You're Emotionally Intuitive** - Because of your empathetic nature, you can quickly tell what someone is feeling without really thinking about it. You're able to instinctively read a person's body language without them having to say a word. When you actively listen to someone tell their story, you're able to take on their pain, their anger, their happiness, or their excitement. You're like an emotional sponge that absorbs the feelings of everyone around you, whether you purposely want to or not.

- **You Immediately Jump At the Chance to Help Others -** Especially when you sense someone in distress. You instantly jump at the chance to help them if it means easing their pain or when you can clearly see how their struggles are impacting them. You relate to what they are going through because it's almost as though you are going through it too. You feel a strong desire to help them take away their pain, so you offer to help them in any way that you can. You give very little thought to the consequences of the emotional toll it takes on you when you're constantly reaching out to help others. The most common consequence is the neglect of your own emotional wellbeing.

- **You Think With Your Heart -** You tend to think with your heart rather than your head. As an empath, the way you do things might not always be logical, but it does tend to come from a place of care and concern. You're compelled to do the loving thing, even if it does not always work in your favor. Since the emotions you feel are so intense, you genuinely care about the other person, and you want to do everything in your power to help them, even at your own expense.

- **You're Sensitive -** Empaths are constantly engulfed in emotions, and it makes you vulnerable. A highly sensitive person is sensitive to many types of energies and reacts emotionally when they feel overstimulated. When a friend of yours is feeling enthusiastic, you share in their exuberance. When someone you care about is distraught, you cry along with them, feeling every bit as hurt and upset as they are. It takes a great deal of energy to feel these emotions, and naturally, they are overwhelming because empaths forget that they have to consider their state of emotions too. Over time, empaths become sensitive to even the slightest emotional change and stressors. Being an empath means you become more susceptible to extreme mood swings because you're so deeply affected by the emotions of others.

- **You Know How to Read People** - Empaths have an uncanny ability to read people and when it comes to understanding other people's motives. They can usually tell when someone is lying or not being authentic. Empaths are highly observant and notice the subtle messages that other people send through their body language and facial expression. They can read other people like an open book.

- **You Can Pickup the Vibe Of A Room** - If you're able to walk into a room and immediately pick up on the energy in that space, chances are you might be an empath. Whether the energy of the room is positive or negative, either way, you're picking up on its signals as soon as you walk through the door.

- **You're A Peacemaker** - Empaths don't like disharmony, for obvious reasons. In the face of conflict, an empath might do one of two things. They could either avoid the situation entirely or try to resolve the issue immediately. They are persistent in finding a solution, and some empaths won't rest until they make sure everyone is happy. They are very sensitive to any form of aggression, even the ones they see online or on the news. They could be moved to tears or feel physically ill watching violence on any kind of media platform.

- **You Are Quirky and Creative -** If you're an empath, you might be culturally creative. Maybe you enjoy painting, making music, singing, or inventing something new, you're inspired to do things that move society forward. Sometimes the ideas you have might not be understood by others or go against the grain, but that doesn't hold you back.

- **You Need Time to Recompose and Recharge Yourself -** Between juggling your own emotions and the emotions of others, you're bound to be emotionally exhausted. Empaths tend to attract people into their lives like magnets because of their gentle and compassionate nature. Being around people is both exhilarating and exhausting for an empath. Alone time becomes a necessity to refuel your emotional gas tank, reset yourself, and gain a sense of balance again. This alone time is necessary at helping to prevent burnout.

- **You Love Nature and Animals -** As an empath, you're more of a lover than a fighter. The love you feel doesn't stop at people alone but extends to animals and nature too. It is not unusual for an empath to feel a deep emotional connection to animals. They probably have a pet or two at home or feel the need to be outdoors often. This is their way of coping and neutralizing the effects of all the emotions they take on from other people. Some empaths prefer to be vegetarian because they connect to the emotions of the animals too.

- **You Tend to Daydream** - Empaths usually make great listeners, but they do have the tendency to daydream during small talk and less important conversations. If you're an empath, one minute you could be listening to a conversation about your friend telling you how their day was at work, and the next minute you'll be thinking about something another person might have said to you earlier. An empath might drift off if a conversation has no strong emotions involved.

- **You're Free-Spirited** - Do you find routines and rules debilitating? Are you free-spirited? Then there's a good chance you might be an empath after all. Even though overstimulation is not a good thing for an empath, you tend to get bored easily if you're not stimulated enough too. You're drawn to adventure, freedom, and travel, and those are the things that make you the happiest.

Is empathy a good thing? Absolutely. It has been proven to be useful in a number of jobs. One example would be if you're in a supervisory position and required to take on the perspectives of others. Actors who possess empathy will also find this skill helpful. Do you relate to any of the signs above? If yes, then chances are you might be an empath.

What Happens When You're an Empath

Is being an empath even a real thing? Or is all of this nothing more than spiritual mumbo-jumbo? It's easy to be dismissive about the whole thing, but the truth is being an empath simply means you're an individual who is highly empathetic. That's it. While other people talk about trying to cultivate the ability to walk a mile in someone else's shoes, empaths can do it for real. Empaths have the ability to go into such an emotional state that other people simply cannot fathom. Does being an empath make you better than a normal person? Not necessarily. An empath is like everyone else, except for the ability to be so highly tuned in to other people's emotions.

Empaths probably had a hard time growing up, or they were commonly misunderstood. Especially when you're growing up in a world today that repeatedly tells us it is *not okay* to be emotional. That it is *not okay* to show your emotions. That you need to bottle those emotions up and keep a stiff upper lip. It's hard to fine-tune your ability to manage your emotions, especially when you're a growing child or teenager who might not fully understand this gift that you possess just yet. It can feel isolating and lonely, and it can feel like no one understands you. When you're an empath:

- **You Connect With Yourself Better** - Before you can begin understanding others, you must first connect with yourself. An effective empath is someone who is centered, someone who is down to earth and grounded. When you are connected with yourself, you're less likely to become distracted easily by what's going on around you. You're able to focus on what matters at hand. It's easy to let our thoughts and emotions get the best of us. It is so easy to be consumed by negativity. Learning to become an empath begins within you, and you start by learning how to focus and gain control of what's happening internally. One of the best techniques you could apply to connect with yourself is through meditation. Meditation helps you find balance, calm, and inner peace, and it can be utilized in almost every aspect of your life whenever you feel anxious, worried or stressed. Learning to control our minds is one of the most difficult things we can do. But to become an empath, this is what is needed. Another method you could use to connect with yourself is spending a few minutes every day just being in your own company. We live in a society today that is far too attached to their mobile devices, and it is time we ditched them for a bit. You'll never connect with yourself if your eyes are constantly glued to a digital screen. Pause, take a breathe, slow down and just appreciate being with yourself. This can be done along with your meditational sessions. It gives you time to reflect on what matters to you, and more importantly, it gives you a few minutes to clear your head and think.

- **You're Focused on the Other Person More Than Yourself** - As an empath, life is less about yourself and more about the other people in it. When you're eating that delicious lunch you just bought from the store nearby, do you think about the people who worked hard to prepare it for you? The hours that they spent in the kitchen, so you didn't have to? When you're enjoying your delicious cup of coffee at the local coffee shop, do you think about the ones who went through all that trouble to gather the coffee beans that you're enjoying right now? The people who helped to ship and deliver that coffee to the local shop where you're sitting at this moment enjoying the fruits of their labor? These people do not necessarily have to be directly in front of you for you to make the connection. It is about taking a moment to think about these people and silently offer a quick thank you, to feel grateful for the people who have made it possible for you to enjoy the little luxuries you have. It is about connecting with humanity.

- **You Walk a Mile in Another's Shoes -** This is perhaps the most obvious thing that you can do, but it works. Being an empath will teach you to see beyond your own feelings and to be able to connect to someone else without prejudice or judgment. Whenever you're involved in a conversation with someone, always picture what it would be like to see things from their point of view, not just yours. This is one of the most basic, yet effective ways, which you can begin growing your empathy skills. We may not realize it, but rarely do we ever give proper thought to what someone else might be going through. We may listen to what they're telling us, and we may sympathize. But how often do we *attempt to feel* what they're currently dealing with? That's what happens when we lack the necessary empathy skills to respond appropriately. It may be silly or dramatic to us, but they to them it could be a very serious matter.

- **Your Curiosity Grows** - Empaths nurture their curiosity. They look for reasons to engage with people they normally wouldn't connect with. Strike up conversations with people who come from different backgrounds than you do. By socializing with a diverse group of individuals and casting your net far and wide, you develop a universal understanding of the world and the people around you. It helps you to see these individuals as humans and break down any further barriers which might have existed that prevented you from being more empathetic with them.

- **You Are No Longer Prejudice** - When someone of a different race, gender, or religion approaches you, how do you react if it is something you're unfamiliar with? Do you automatically set up a barrier? That's being prejudice. For some, being prejudice is already an innate part of who they are, but not for an empath. When you are an empath, you are going to have to challenge your prior beliefs, the prejudices you currently have. Work to get rid of them and start to view people, places, and situations with an open mind. Just because a person is different from you doesn't mean you should be wary. Everyone is still human at the end of the day. We're all equals on this earth and we should mutually respect one another. To help you with this, try to find something which you can connect on. Some common ground. When you can relate to them and connect on a shared interest, you'll have greater interactive experiences and eventually, boundaries will just slip away. This is when greater empathy occurs, by opening up to the people around you and welcoming them as part of your circle.

Empathy is a gift. There is always a reason for every reaction, and it is empathy that is going to help you see past the difficult behavior someone may be displaying towards you and take it a step further. There may be moments in your life when the emotions become so overwhelming you wish you didn't have this ability. That you wish you could be normal. Being an empath is not just about the passive receiving of emotion. Being an empath is not about being a hopelessly sensitive person who is battered by the emotions of others all the time. If you think about it, being an empath is almost like a *superpower*. Imagine being so connected to another human being beyond what others are capable of. Theoretically, if you know exactly what someone else is feeling, you should be able to know exactly how to comfort them, although admittedly, this does take practice. As an empath, you're in a powerful position of being able to relate to emotions and use them to your advantage. By developing an understanding of your emotions and the emotions of others, you are in a unique position to reach out and recognize that empathy is necessary for forming deep, meaningful relationships that are mutually beneficial. An empath knows how to appropriately respond and manage a situation because they are able to empathize with the people that they are speaking to. Empathy is a quality that is going to help you start developing even greater interpersonal and social skills, and this is how great leaders are able to influence change in the people that they manage under their care.

When empathy is combined with social skills, it will help transform the way that you relate to the people around you. For a leader to be able to forge good working relationships with their team members, they need to have good social skills about them. For you to maintain healthy, everyday relationships with the people who matter most in your life, you need empathy and good social skills to work with. Poor social skills have been known to be one of the main causes that arguments and misunderstandings happen because one or both parties have reacted poorly in the situation. As an empath, you can avoid all of this using your superpower. Instead of getting frustrated with the way that they are behaving, empathy will make you reach out towards them and ask them if they are really ok. Empathy will help you get to the root cause of the problem, and when you're able to anticipate someone else's needs because you can recognize the emotional symptoms that they're displaying, that's when you effectively become an agent of change. Walking a mile in someone else's shoes can do a lot to help you change your perspective.

Empathy and self-awareness will make you a much better person in a social setting. When you begin to develop an understanding of the emotions of those around you, you begin to find ways of relating to them on a more personal level. When you're viewed as someone who is easy to connect with, someone who is easy to talk to, people will automatically start to draw closer to you in a social setting because they feel comfortable being in your presence. Other people sometimes have painful emotions they need to deal with, and in times like these, they need someone to lean on. A shoulder to cry on. Someone who can listen to them without judgment and without prejudice. Someone who can make them feel better by just being *there*, even if that is all that they do. Displaying empathy towards others does not mean you're accepting of their less than desirable behavior, but rather empathy is there to serve as a reminder that everyone has their own troubles that they are dealing with. We often get so caught up in our own troubles and worries that we don't even consider the difficulties that someone else might be facing. If your colleague is going through a bad day and reacting harshly towards the rest of the team, empathy is the quality that helps you understand they have troubles too. Empathy will be the reason that you find some time to pull them aside and ask if everything is okay instead of getting worked up and irritated towards them because of the way that they're behaving. That is what it means to be an empath.

THE SCIENCE BEHIND IT

IN LIFE, we are faced with all sorts of challenges, and we desperately need each other to see things through. We need to be able to rely on each other, support each other, be there for each other, and empathize with each other during the most challenging moments of our lives. Challenges are never easy, but knowing that you're not going through it alone can make life a little more bearable and that's why being an empath makes you special. You're in a very unique position where your gift can prove to be a blessing in the lives of those who may need it. But is there more to empathy than just emotions? Is there actual science behind it?

The Science Behind Being an Empath

Empathy has been a part of our human emotional range for as long as we can remember. From the days of our early ancestors, in fact. We did not have survival abilities like claws are being able to leap from the tall branches of a tree to stay alive. We survived because we had this one, superpower on our side: *We had the ability to imagine what another person might be feeling.* This allowed us to work really well in groups and gave us the ability to form societies and empires. Humans are social creatures by nature, and without empathy, we would not have survived long as a species if we did not have this innate ability to feel someone else's emotions and genuinely want to help them.

Empathy may sound like a wishy-washy philosophy, but it is not. Far from it, in fact. Neuroscientists discovered what is known as the *Empathy Circuit*. This circuit was first discovered when the group of neuroscientists was working with patients who had dementia. These patients had a particular kind of dementia, which was referred to as *frontotemporal dementia* or FTD for short. One of the side effects of battling FTD was the patients started losing their ability to care. They don't care about their children, their lovers, their spouses, their family, their friends. Not caring about the significant people in your life is when the breakdown of everything that makes you human begins. The human connection is part of our unique makeup, and losing that ability to care and connect with others is like losing a part of ourselves. Patients dealing with FTD had certain parts of their brain shutting down, which indicated where in the brain empathy was supposed to be. That's how the empathy circuit was discovered.

Certain circuits in the brain are wired to help us detect emotions and then produce an appropriate emotional response to it. For example, certain parts of the *amygdala* and the *temporal pole* are important in helping us better understand the emotions and experiences that someone else might be going through. These experiences will then project to the *anterior cingulate cortex* of the brain, which generates this emotional reaction throughout the body through our autonomic nervous system and our face. This will, in turn, will trigger the *interior insula* portion of the brain, which is the part of the brain that helps us represent our internal states. It's not enough to have the brain working to produce the emotional reaction that we feel; our brain also needs to represent how the body has responded and monitor those internal cues.

The *Empathy Circuit* is powerful. Imagine for a minute that you're hanging out with a friend. Your friend is telling you about something terrible that happened to them this week and they are visibly distressed over the matter. As you're listening to them, your brain picks up on their emotions, and you begin to empathize. This feeling is triggered throughout your body by the brain, and the more you empathize with them, the more your entire body starts to get in sync with theirs. Your mirror their facial expressions, their posture, their heartbeat and even breathing. You start to take this a step further by reaching out and trying to comfort your friend and it works. Your friend starts to feel better as the two of you work on ideas and brainstorm solutions and suggestions about how to weather the storm, or you've helped by simply being the listening ear that your friend needed to vent their emotions. Now, can you imagine what would happen in this same situation if you *did not* empathize with your friend? Aside from probably causing your friend to feel more upset than they already did, you've probably done some damage to that friendship by not reacting in the appropriate manner expected. Especially when the two of you are supposed to be friends. The less empathetic you are, the more closed off you eventually start to become. Eventually, you'll reach a point where you're cold, distant, and aloof.

Relationships are a big part of who we are, even if you may be an introvert. Even introverts reach out to the people they trust and care about every now and then. It is *impossible* to survive this world without any kind of relationship or connection at all. Empathy is in our nature, and it is unfortunate that the world we live in today is weakening the internal empathy circuit we all have. We're so obsessed and distracted with what's happening in the digital world and social media that we forget to pay attention to what is happening right in front of us. The more connected we become to the digital world, the more disconnected we become to our fellow human beings. Being divided is only going to make it more difficult to come together to resolve problems and work together when we need to because we've lost the ability to do it. Unless it's behind a keyboard or computer screen, we've forgotten what it means to make a real connection because that part of our brain has shrunk from a lack of use. Yes, areas of the brain will shrink when they are underused. The activities we engage in creates changes in brain structure and rewires our neural circuits by eliminating the connections we don't use that often while simultaneously strengthening the ones we do.

The good news? If it can be shrunk, it can be *strengthened too*. Yes, our empathy circuits can be strengthened, and it begins with exercise. The exercise begins when you notice you're feeling negatively toward someone. Like when someone cuts you off in traffic as you're rushing to get home. This makes you angry and you notice this emotion. First, take a deep breath until you once again feel in control of your thoughts. Now, take the emotional state you fee a step further and try to understand *why* this person did what they did. Maybe they were rushing too. Maybe there's an emergency at home and they're in a hurry to get there. Maybe they've had a long day at work and they're distracted, not really thinking about the other people on the road. There could be a million reasons why they did what they did. You don't need to guess the right answer and you probably never will. But the act of trying to understand *why* the other person reacted the way they did is an exercise in strengthening your empathy circuit. You don't have to love everyone, but you can almost always empathize with them if you tried.

Empath Benefits

We all have the ability to empathize with others, but *empaths* take this to a whole new extreme level. Empaths can actually feel the emotions of others, whether they want to or not. It is something that happens so naturally that some empaths don't even realize when they're started to take on someone else's emotions. It just happens. Like a sponge that immediately soaks up what it comes into contact with. They don't have a choice in the emotions either, and whether what they pick up on is positive or negative, empaths are going to feel it as soon as they are within the space or in close contact with the person. That is some pretty powerful stuff. Yes, being an empath can be overwhelming, especially when you're flooded with multiple emotions at once. But there are benefits to this, and these benefits are the reason why empathy is a gift, even though sometimes it can feel like a curse.

Here's a mantra to start keeping in mind: *Empathy is your superpower.* Your highly sensitive state is going to allow you to be in a heightened state of awareness to other people and your surroundings. You have a greater capacity, capability, and awareness of yourself and others. It allows you to quickly shift and change the state that you're in too. This means if you're in a situation where you're feeling stressed, depressed, or anxious, you have the ability to shift your mental, emotional, and physical state if you want it to.

Empaths have an extremely reactive neurological system. They don't have the same filters that other people do to block out stimulation, which explains why they often feel overwhelmed by the energies and the emotions around them. Empaths are certainly a special group of people, although this ability does come with certain challenges, once you understand what a little more about your ability, the challenges become easier to deal with. Here are some other benefits that come with this superpower:

- **You Have the Makings Of A Good Leader -** Ambitious individuals stand to benefit the most from having empathy as a skill. In a leadership position, you will be responsible for several other individuals who are looking to you to set an example and to provide guidance. All eyes will be on you, and your relationships with those under your care are going to determine your success, your failure as a leader. Empathy-driven leaders use all five components of EI to help them build better bonds with people they work with; they use self- awareness, and self-regulation to tune in to what and how everyone else is feeling, and to assess the strengths and weakness of the team of people they're working with. They rely on their social skills and empathy to connect with these individuals and see things from their perspective. This is what separates a great leader from a mediocre one.

- **You Become Socially Adept -** Empathy will make you a much better person in a social setting. When you begin to develop an understanding of the emotions of those around you, you begin to find ways of relating to them on a more personal level. When you're viewed as someone who is easy to connect with, someone who is easy to talk to, people will automatically start to draw closer to you in a social setting because they feel comfortable being in your presence.

- **Your Relationship Get Better -** Our life is all about relationships. The relationships that we have are what define us, what motivates us, and what can either drive us towards success or hold us back. Some relationships in our lives are more permanent, such as the ones we have with our families, friends, children, partners or spouses, and there are some relationships who may or may not be around for a certain period of time, like the ones we may have with our colleagues, roommates, and acquaintances. With every relationship, especially the ones that matter, you want to keep it as healthy as possible. Toxic relationships can quickly bring you down, and if you constantly let your emotions get in the way of your actions, you could be that toxic relationship. A damaged relationship is not always easy to repair, and to avoid damaging it at all in the first place, you need to have EI on your side.

- **You Treat Everyone with Kindness -** Empaths treat everyone with kindness because they have empathy and social skills. They are able to empathize even with difficult people and try to see things from their perspective to understand the reason for their behavior. You're also a lot more respectful towards people. Respect is a vital habit towards cultivating happiness in your relationships that you seek. Each time that you show disrespect towards anyone, you are in a way letting them know that you don't accept them for the way that they are. Remember that people are unique individuals, just like you are, and part of cultivating relationships is accepting others and valuing them for who they are, not who you expect them to be.

- **You Have the Ability to Develop Connections -** Because you feel what others are experiencing, it gives you the ability to forge connections very quickly. Empaths also tend to exhibit their empathy in a subconscious way that promotes true, heartfelt connections. Sometimes without even saying a word. This encourages others to open up and share their vulnerabilities, maybe even confide in empaths in a way they would not feel comfortable doing with other people. Empaths are great at being such active listeners that people naturally gravitate towards them. This ability to forge deep connections could lead to stronger trust in the relationships that have been built, and this is an ability not everyone is privileged to have. Making any kind of real-life connection these days has become a challenge since social media and technology came into the picture, let alone a lasting, meaningful connection the way an empath can.

- **You Develop a Stronger Connection With Loved Ones -** You might say that your connection with your loved ones is almost telepathic. You understand the people you love the most in a way that no one else does. At times, you may experience a sudden emotion or pain, even if they are not right next to you at the time. That's how strong of a connection you can forge with them. Your intuition when it comes to your loved ones is strong and you tend to follow that implicitly, and as an empath, you pay attention to your intuition more than other people do.

- **You Tend to Be a Planner -** Being a planner can be a good thing since it stops you from rushing to make impulsive decisions. As an empath, you see deep meaning in certain situations, and you're able to assess what the emotional outcomes of each possible situation may be. You spend more time planning your next course of action to avoid rushing into a decision. Empaths prefer to choose the best course of action with the least resistance since they don't want to add to their emotional burden if they can avoid it.

- **You're More Forgiving -** Gandhi once said that *"forgiveness is something that is attributed to the strong."* He was right. That is exactly what empaths are. It takes great strength to take on someone else's emotions. It's not as easy as it might seem and neither is forgiveness. Forgiveness is one of the most powerful tools you could possess and coming from the perspective of an empath, it is much easier to forgive when you have the ability to see things from someone else's perspective. Not only will you eventually gain the ability to forgive others over time, but you'll also learn to forgive yourself. You'll learn acceptance, and you'll learn how to be much happier when you let go of all the unnecessary emotions that reside within you.

- **You Get Better at Naming Your Emotions -** Another great exercise that is going to enhance your self-awareness abilities is to name your feelings. Instead of just generalizing by saying I am feeling happy, define that emotion in greater detail. What level of happiness are you feeling? Cheerful? Joyful? You understand your emotions so well that you understand what triggered that reaction within you and then take a step back, assess the way you reacted at that moment, and think about how you might have reacted better in such a situation.

The Side Effects You Have to Live With As an Empath

One mistake many beginner empaths make when they are first learning to recognize their ability as a gift is that these beginner empaths believe they are less worthy than others might be. Especially in today's world where being overly emotional or sensitive is perceived negatively. Of course, this scenario could work both ways. Beginner empaths might start to believe that they are *better* than everyone else because they're got this gift. Either belief is common for many empaths who are starting to fully understand the unique perspective that comes with this ability. You might have experienced either one of these scenarios at some point or another. If you do notice either scenario might be the way you're feeling right now, don't judge yourself. Give yourself permission to notice it, acknowledge the way you feel. Remember this is part of the human experience. Right now, what you need to do is try not to tip the scales to either extreme. Feel too inferior, and you might impact your self-esteem while feeling too special or superior might lead you down the path of unhealthy narcissism.

Like everything else in life, being an empath has inevitable side effects. Like being constantly exhausted, for example, which is a side effect of being an empath that you might not have realized if you never noticed you had the gift. Empaths feel everything deeply and intensely, and that kind of intensity is not without its implications. Being an empath is something not many people can relate to. It's a feeling you get in your gut. If you've been able to relate to anything that has been talked about so far in this book, then your gut feeling is right, and you most likely have the gift. People rely on empaths for emotional healing, guidance, and support. But not many people think about the implications of what it means to bear the emotional burden of others. The darker side effects of being an empath can be both painful and harrowing to carry.

Here are some of the side effects of being an empath you might not have realized:

- **Sometimes It's Hard to Control Your Emotions** - If you find yourself losing control of your emotions far too often, getting emotionally carried away in situations that have no real cause for it, that's one of the side effects that come with being an empath. This can get better with emotional intelligence. Difficulty controlling emotions will make it hard for you to manage relationships too. Friendships, relationships with your family, colleagues, even your kids. Without the necessary social skills, empathy, and self-awareness, you're going to find it very hard to maintain any kind of lasting relationship in your life.

- **You Feel Tired and Demotivated** - You find yourself lacking the desire to do anything, even if it is something as small as checking and responding to your emails. You feel drained, tired, and demoralized all the time, especially after an encounter with anyone who might be harboring toxic emotions. Since empaths can understand people on a deeper emotional level, they feel it is their duty to listen and help others and when they fail to achieve that, they feel tired and demotivated.

- **You Feel the Need to Make the World A Better Place -** A lot of empaths believe that their purpose is to help make the world a better place. They feel an overwhelming desire to bring positive change, and this desire is second to none. Sure, other people may get the occasional thought of making a difference in the world, but empaths feel this desire within their very being and they are driven by it because they identify so deeply with the negativity around them.

- **You Feel Overwhelmed By What Others View As "Normal"** - Empaths are highly sensitive individuals, and because of their nature, what is considered normal to others might be overwhelming to them. Extreme sensitivity is not an exaggeration. Imagine an emotion that you're feeling right now, like sadness. Now, imagine feeling the intensity of that sadness by 10 times more. That intense feeling can cause a great deal of stress for someone who is deeply affected by it.

- **You Find It Difficult to Separate Yourself From Others** - The hallmark of being an empath is your ability to feel and experience other people's emotions. As an empath, this awareness could result in a difficulty separating yourself from others because of the tendency to take on their burden and their pain as your own. Since an empath is an emotional sponge, if they're not careful, they can absorb the negative energies of others and take them on as their own. For a lot of empaths, joy and happiness come from helping others to heal. That's why they are referred to as emotional healers of the world. But the dark side of this desire is that they become so caught up in healing other people that they forget to heal themselves.

- **You Might Have Complex Emotions Yourself** - It's easy to think that empaths have their life together and forget that they have problems of their own too. A lot of empaths have complex emotions and issues that they are secretly dealing with too. They may have the gift of helping others go through difficult situations, but that does not mean the life of an empath is all sunshine and rainbows either. Some empaths struggle with problems like depression, anxiety, low self-esteem, and depression. They feel intense emotions daily, and this is bound to impact them in one way or another. If empaths are not careful, this high-intensity of emotions they feel every day can lead to self-destruction. Empaths who don't know how to deal with these challenges turn to addictive activities like smoking or consuming hard substances as a way to deal with the negative issues they are going through in their lives.

- **You Might Have Difficulty Falling In Love** - Most empaths have tried loving before, but their kind nature has left them hurt or preyed upon by others. Empaths are capable of loving to a fault, so much that they are sometimes exploited for their kindness. After a while, falling in love becomes difficult because it makes them wary of pain and disappointment. Like other people, they are afraid of being hurt again and may eventually have difficulty opening up to the idea of love. They hold back a piece of their heart and avoid falling in love too deeply to avoid putting themselves at risk of being hurt again.

- **You Neglect Yourself** - Empaths are givers rather than receivers. The challenge is that in doing so, they are prone to neglect themselves and their needs. They give up so much of themselves to make sure people around them are happy, but they receive nothing in return. Whenever value or energy is handed out without being replenished, sooner or later, the source is going to get dried up. In this case, the empath is the source. This is exactly what will happen if they neglect themselves for too long.

Being an empath is wonderful, but the painful dark side can sometimes feel like a burden that is too much to bear.

The Unforeseen Toxicity

Your desire to help others as an empath could leave you more open and vulnerable to being taken advantage of by toxic people. Unfortunately, these toxic personalities are only going to create more unnecessary drama in your life. This is the unforeseen toxicity, one that is going to leave you feeling miserable because toxic personalities are nothing more than a drain on your energy. Toxic personalities will never be truly happy, no matter what you do for them. There will always be a reason to complain, a reason why it is never good enough. They will hold you back and weigh you down in life, diminishing your confidence and belief in yourself. It can be difficult to leave once you've formed a bond with them, especially if you care about them. It is difficult to break free from the chain of narcissistic abuse that will be inflicted on you by these manipulators. Do you know why? Because they *don't* care about you. The only agenda they care about is their own.

But learning to recognize them at the beginning for who they are is how to learn to avoid them in the future. Have you ever been so frustrated or bothered by someone's behavior that even thinking about them is enough to get you worked up and exasperated? Even when they are not around? That' what a toxic personality can do to you. The most dangerous thing about them is how much power they have over your emotions, especially if you're an empath. A toxic person can be so powerful that they can inflict feelings of anger and frustration just by being themselves. If this is how you feel each time you encounter someone toxic, you are giving them power over your emotions. Each time they invoke a strong reaction from you, they have power over your life because you let them bother you to that extent. Replaying a toxic encounter in your mind is letting that toxic person have power over you. Even when they are not around, they are occupying your thoughts. The more you think about them, the more precious time you are giving them time, which they do not deserve. The more you try to help them, the more they will take advantage of you. It's in their nature. Letting a toxic person occupy your thoughts means you are letting them steal your valuable time, and this is precisely why they are so toxic and should be kept as far away as possible.

There is also a very real danger that empaths might get into relationships with toxic personalities, and this can be a real breeding ground for self-destruction. Narcissists and manipulative personalities love to prey on the benevolence and generosity of empaths. These narcissists know that empaths full of energy and positive vibes and this is what they prey on. Relationships like these are parasitic, where the narcissist ends up benefiting while the empath ends up feeling drained or hurt. Toxic people have a way of getting into people's heads and messing with their confidence. If you let them, they will hold you back because they prevent you from living your life to the fullest. Misery loves company, and so does a toxic person. They will do their best to make you feel as bad as they do, and they do it by making you feel like you are "stuck" without better options. Passive-aggressiveness could make an appearance here, where the toxic person would rely on this tactic to make you feel that you are incapable of moving forward and that you have no choice but to remain where you are with them.

It is crucial for empaths to acknowledge that narcissism is a disorder. By continuing to support the narcissist, you are either knowingly or unknowingly supporting a lie. The person you *think* you are helping does not exist. This can be a hard pill to swallow for the empath, and it is heartbreaking to know that there are unscrupulous individuals out there who will prey on their kindness in this manner. The narcissist is *not a tortured soul you need to help.* They don't need your special kind of love. They are demanding, judgemental, manipulative and ungrateful, always projecting their own selfish needs and feelings unto everyone else. They will have you trapped in an endless vicious cycle that will keep repeating on a loop unless you cut them out of your life once and for all. No matter how much you show them your deep, conditional love, they are never going to change for the better unless there is an internal motivation within them to do it. The sad truth is, narcissists are morally bankrupt individuals who will never appreciate the things other people do for them. Instead, they feel entitled to any love and devotion that is directed to them.

If only everyone in the world could be a little more like empaths, what a better utopian world it would be. Sadly, that is far from the truth. Most people today are so consumed with their own issues we have forgotten how to empathize with the people around us. To bring balance back into your life after an encounter with a toxic individual requires you to surround yourself with people who are the complete opposite. People who inspire you, you radiate positivity, you encourage you, and help you reach your full potential are the people you want to seek out. People who make you happy. Oprah Winfrey is a big advocate of this method, and she constantly reminds her followers to only surround themselves with people who are going to lift. them up higher. Dear empaths, if you have done everything in your power to help the people around you, then take comfort in that fact. Sometimes all you can do is your best and hope that it is good enough.

TYPES OF EMPATHS

IS THIS A GIFT? Or a curse? If you're an empath, that thought has probably crossed your mind on more than one occasion. If you're struggling to find the balance between your emotions and that of others you take on, being an empath may seem like a curse. One of the emotions you're going to frequently feel from others is hurt. Maybe you've been labeled "hurt" or "overly emotional" by others who did not understand your abilities. In the beginning, you probably struggled with understanding yourself and why you feel emotions so strongly.

Reasons Why Being an Empath Is a Gift

You're a *healer*. As an empath, it is almost like you're bequeathed with a special mission to heal and help others, some of whom might not even realize they need help. Not a lot of people are walking this earth on a mission to heal other people emotionally and psychologically. You're one of the unique few with the power to make a genuine difference in someone's life. You could be the reason between hope and despair. You have a purpose in this world where so many others struggle to find purpose or even meaning to their lives. You have an ingenuity, skill, and a tireless ability to take on the energy of others, heal those that need, and still be a ray of hope for many who need a shoulder to cry on. Your gift is a *blessing*. *You are a blessing,* and it is time to start believing that. Like all gifts, not everything is going to be perfect and smooth sailing all the time. There will be moments when you experience highs and others when you feel so low you wish you never had this ability.

There's a reason why empathy is one of the core skills of emotional intelligence. It is the skill you need to comfort a grieving friend, understand someone else's point of view, persuade others to agree with you (in a non-manipulative way), diffuse tension, and find solutions to problems. In a complicated and stressful world, your gift is appreciated by the many lives you've helped to make a difference in, and you know this because you can *feel* their gratitude. Empathy is the glue that holds relationships together. While no doubt being an empath is overwhelming, it doesn't make it any less of a gift. No one understands the world and the people in it quite like you do.

For all these reasons and the reasons listed below, this is why your empathetic abilities should be considered a gift:

- **You See People As They Are** - You see the good, the bad, and everything in between. You see the emotions that they struggle to express. You see the pain they are so desperately trying to hide. Your ability to see beyond what's right in front of you means you see the potential in others where those who are not empaths might be quick to dismiss. You don't judge the person immediately, but instead, you try to understand the *reason* behind their emotions and actions. You question why they act the way they do and you try to find ways to help them. You know there is more to the story and you believe in the good in people. You're not quick to dismiss others without giving them the benefit of the doubt, and these are just some of the many reasons why the people you have helped love you so much. You're a unique spirit and the lives you touch are forever changed because you see people as they are.

- **You Don't Need Words to Be Expressive -** The accepted belief is that effective communication can only occur when two or more people are engaged in meaningful back and forth conversation. For an empath, communication can happen even without words. It is possible for an empath to merely sit with a friend and loved one, not say a word but somehow make them feel better. Some empaths can even read the minds of the people they are closest to, an ability that a lot of people would consider "weird" or "freaky." But it's not weird or freaky at all. It's because you are so attuned to the emotional vibrations of others. You think about them rather than focus on yourself.

- **You Have the Power to Heal -** Your ability to heal is your most significant attribute. It is a superpower that you have. Your ability to heal is so unique that in some cases, your presence alone is enough to bring a smile to someone's face when they are feeling down. Empaths also have this uncanny ability to actively listen, which is in itself a tremendous healing power. Active listening is an ability that requires you to be *fully present* in the conversation. When empaths actively listen, they are giving the other person their undivided attention. The easiest way to show someone you accept them, and you're open and willing to listen to what they have to say is to simply show them you're listening. How? Through non-verbal cues and make it apparent you're listening intently, like what an empath does. Encourage them to keep sharing their ideas without interrupting them or breaking the conversational flow by showing your support using non-verbal cues. Nod along in agreement when something they've said resonates with you. Maintain good eye contact throughout, have a friendly smile, or the appropriate emotional reaction on your face. These are all skills that come naturally to an empath and it is all part of their healing magic.

- **You Have the Ability to Read Auras -** Empaths that are extremely in tune with their gift have the ability to read auras. There are three types of people in the world: *The good buys, the bad guys, and the people who possess what can only be described as ugly personalities.* Some empaths have the power to see which category a person belongs too because they can read auras. An aura is described as the human energy field, and some believe that this energy field comes in different colors that emanate around a person. Sometimes not just a person, but it could also be present around an animal or even an inanimate object for that matter. Not everyone has the ability to see auras just like that on their own. Usually, it is psychics who claim to have that gift, and they are able to go as far as seeing the size, color, and the vibration intensity that is generated by a person's aura. Empaths can do it too. This ethereal radiation surrounds each living being, and it usually surrounds them within the space of two or three feet around the body. Most people are consumed by only believing and seeing what is directly in front of them that oftentimes they forget there is a whole other spiritual world out there that they are completely overlooking. But not you, because your empathic abilities give you the gift of being able to see a person's true intentions by reading their aura.

- **You Can Immediately Sense When Something Is Wrong -** Even with strangers. You don't have to be best friends with a person to know when something is not right. While other people are only able to develop a sixth sense about the people whom they consistently stay in contact with, you as an empath, have the ability to do this with *everyone*. Even complete strangers. Your ability to read others is not based on a relationship bias, but rather it is based on your gift of being able to immediately tune in to the emotions within your range.

- **You're Innate Creative Ability -** As an empath, you have a second gift of innate creativity. Most empaths are highly creative individuals who can transform plans and ideas and turn them into reality. There are certain industries in which empaths flourish well, such as fields of work that include art and design, marketing, and communication.

- **You Have the Powers of Persuasion** - The ability to read and sense the emotions of others puts you in a unique position. You have the ability to persuade others to see your point of view, believe in your ideas, and see things from your point of view when you're trying to reach an amicable agreement or diffuse an argument. Trying to convince, persuade, or change someone's mind is challenging. Perhaps the problem lies with the approach that we use. Most people tend to lead with their own point of view and their own perspectives and then proceed to point out what the other party needs to do to change. This approach hardly ever works the way we intend it to because it makes the other party defensive, even personally attacked when they're being told all the ways that they're "wrong" and why they need to "change" according to you. This is where your gift comes in handy. Being sensitive to your surroundings and the people in it means you're always going to be considerate of other people's feelings and you'll do your best to ensure all parties involved reach an agreement that everyone is happy with.

- **You Can Inspire Others** - Your empathetic nature can be used to inspire others to practice self-love and kindness towards themselves and others. You can inspire others by showing them how to be loving, caring, and giving, and treating everyone with kindness by being an example of what they should do. During hard times, your gift is going to be a beacon of hope for those who need to know that there is still love and kindness in the world. Among all the communication skills we can develop, empathic listening skills is one of the most valuable ones in our efforts to foster meaningful, deep connections with others. The ability to listen with compassion, demonstrate kindness for the plight of others, to be patient, loving, and accepting is a skill that not a lot of people possess these days. Therefore, to find someone with these rare attributes is like finding a diamond in the rough, and it is this very individual who is capable of becoming the master of both their professional and personal interactions. Simple acts of kindness will go a long way, and they will be remembered.

- **You're More Flexible in Relationships -** Successful relationships happen when there's an equal balance of give and take. Empaths are able to easily build connections and handle conversations effortlessly by being approachable, dependable, and caring. In most of the relationships that are formed, an empath's love and kindness are reciprocated equally unless they, unfortunately, encounter manipulative or toxic personalities.

- **You Can Expand Your Thoughts -** An empath is blessed with the ability to see beyond what other people can see. While others have a narrow, closed-off view of the world, empaths do not. You see beyond what is in front of you, and you make an effort to understand the perspectives and points of view of others. In doing so, you become intellectually and emotionally rich, which helps you take your communication abilities to the next level. No matter who you may be talking to, there is something to be learned from every encounter.

- **You Are Humble -** Stepping into someone else's shoes can be a very humbling experience. Most people believe their lives are hard until they encounter someone else who has it *much harder* than they do. Even then, they will not be able to fully comprehend the difficulty of the challenges that a person may be facing. They may sympathize, but they will never be able to empathize in a way the empath can. If you're an empath, this is why your gift is such a unique blessing. You understand others so well because you *literally* feel their pain, and this allows you to put away your judgments and assumptions. You're humbled by the emotions that you feel, and this trait is especially useful when you're dealing with difficult people. Difficult people want to be understood just as much as everyone else, and you have the power to do it. People open up to you when they see you're coming from a place of true intent to understand their perspective, rather than a malicious one.

Being an empath might make you feel like you are compelled to help everyone you meet, but that's not true. You *always* have a choice. You may get along well with a lot of people, but you still get to choose the kind of people you want to help and interact with at the end of the day. Whether you want to help them or not, it is still your choice; you don't have to feel forced into doing it because of your special ability. You still have a duty to protect your well-being and your emotions, and you need to take care of yourself first before you can take care of someone else. When necessary, you can always take a step back and disconnect from their energy so you don't have to feel overwhelmed

Identifying the Types of Empaths

Empaths are among the most beautiful souls around because of their naturally loving and caring personalities. The beauty of being human is how we are all unique and special in our own way, even empaths. Not all empaths are built equal. They come in all shapes, sizes, and with varying degrees of abilities. Understanding the type of empath you are can help you make the most of your ability. If you believe you have empathic abilities, you might resonate with one of the types of empath categories listed below:

- **Emotional Empaths -** These individuals are deeply affected by the emotions of others. They have an uncanny ability to connect with the people around them and feel what they are going through. Being very people-oriented individuals, it is not uncommon for the emotional empath to put the needs of others ahead of their own.

- **Spiritual Empaths -** Emotional empaths connect with people in the physical world, and spiritual empaths connect with the spiritual world. They are sometimes referred to as *Medium Empaths,* and have a deep connection with spirits, with the dead, and figures of the spiritual world. Although they may be present in the physical world, spiritual empaths have a mind that tends to wander because they relate with a world that is beyond this one. Some empaths serve as a medium between the spiritual and the physical world, sort of like what psychics do.

- **Physical Empaths -** They are like emotional empaths, with the ability to sense the emotional pain of others. Except that physical empaths can also sense *physical* pain, a person might be experiencing in their body. They thrive as natural healers since they have the ability to detect which areas of the body a person might be in need of healing.

- **Intuitive Empaths -** These empaths receive information from others by merely being around them. The more they connect with the person, the more they get to know the difficulties and challenges faced by the person without being told. They rely on intuition to decipher the hidden meaning and cues behind the body language and facial expressions exhibited.

- **Geometric Empaths -** They're also called environmental empaths. These empaths are deeply connected to the world around them, and they receive signals and energy about their physical environment. These empaths can read the energy and signals that are transmitted by rocks, soil, air, or water. Some empaths are even able to recognize when bad weather or some form of a natural disaster may be happening, an ability that is shared by animals. Animals always know before a natural disaster strikes and they run to higher ground and seek shelter even before it happens. Geometric empaths have the same ability. They're happiest when they are surrounded by nature, and find a deep connection to certain places that they feel most comfortable in. Geometric empaths love nature and they love to do what they can to preserve it. It's not uncommon to find in activist groups that advocate against anything that threatens to destroy nature.

- **Precognitive Empaths** - These empaths have the capacity to know what happens *before* it happens. Sometimes they see it in a dream, sometimes they see it in a vision. These visions of future events can be both good and bad. They can sometimes predict a situation or event before it has happened either through dreams or through a strong feeling or emotion they may receive. This strong sense of intuition can be a good thing that is useful in decision-making scenarios.

- **Animal Empaths** - Also sometimes referred to as *Fanna Empaths*. These individuals are drawn to animals so strongly it is almost as though they can communicate with these animals. Such a strong bond exists between these empaths and animals that at times, it almost seems as though the empaths and hear and speak the animal's language. To these empaths, the animals are their best friends, and they are firmly against animal cruelty or abuse of any kind. They are even against killing animals for food and opt to go down the vegan path instead. To them, hurting an animal is sacrilege. *Fanna* empaths thrive in animal-related occupations, and if this sounds like you, then you might be a Fanna empath.

- **Flora Empaths** - These are the floral empaths. You have the empaths who love animals, and you have the empaths you love plants and flowers, which are the *Flora Empaths*. They love greens, and they have the gift of the green thumb. They love spending time outdoors nurturing plants and flowers and planting seeds to grow new crops. They feel refreshed and full of life when they immerse themselves in gardens, parks, or any outdoor space with living things. These empaths are so tuned in to the plants they care for that like the *Fanna* empaths, they seem to hear and speak the language of the plants. They know exactly what a plant needs to grow and they are happiest when they are immersed in an occupation that pursues this course.

- *Heyoka* **Empaths** - The *Heyoka* empaths can sense things about others, know what is going to happen, and sometimes change or influence the course of events to a person's favor. Only a few empaths are considered *Heyoka's*. In Native America, the term *Heyoka* is used to refer to individuals who have the ability to mirror the emotions of others. *Heyoka* empaths see the world differently than other people do. These empaths feel unsettled if there is a problem that is unresolved. Even when they are sleeping, their mind is continually active.

- **Psychometric Empaths -** These empaths have the ability to draw meaning and impressions from objects. They can sense the energy, memories, and significant information from inanimate objects like photographs or jewelry. This information may be received in the form of images and sounds, tastes, aura, or emotions. These empaths are able to sense the past history of an object by touching it.

- **Claircognizant Empaths -** These empaths possess a high level of intuition that allows them to understand the true nature of any situation. These empaths are able to immediately detect when someone may be putting on an act or lying to them. Their intuition is so strong they can assess or read situations better than anyone else, which allows them to gauge exactly what needs to be done in such a situation. This makes them an excellent problem solver and the ones that others turn to when they need help solving a problem.

- **Telepathic Empath -** These empaths have the ability to transmit words, emotions, or images to someone else's mind without physical interaction. It is a form of communication in which thoughts are channeled or exchanged between a sender and receiver. If you are a telepathic empath, you're able to know what others are thinking when you look at them. It's a fantastic ability to have, but it does come with a price. Knowing someone else's thoughts is not always a good thing.

Being an empath can be a bittersweet experience. When you're in the presence of happy emotions, it empowers you and makes you feel happy too. At the same time, when you're in the presence of negative emotions, your ability won't allow you to simply tune out those feelings, and they affect you just as much as the positive ones do. Not all empath categories are also able to sense to see auras. The ability to read auras is a talent that not many people possess. If you are an empath who can, this is an added bonus to your existing gift. It is intriguing to find out things about the people around you that they wouldn't necessarily want to reveal on their own, and you can combine this information with what you're able to sense from their emotions. The ability to read auras is like having your very own personal in-built lie detector test. You will always be able to tell what the other person is thinking or feeling, even if they are pretending to cover it up or trying to hide it.

Being able to so acutely read people is going to be very beneficial to you because you will be able to take control of the situation at hand and guide it in the direction that you want it to go. Remember, auras reveal a person's intentions for what they really are, and having the ability to read auras will also put you in better control of your own body, your health, your emotions, everything you need to become a better version of yourself.

How to Make the Most Out of Your Gift

Once you've figured out you're an empath, the next question to think about would be what you can do to develop this ability so you can make the most out of your gift. To become a better, stronger, and more empowered empath, there are several things you need to do first:

*S*tep 1: Avoid Judgment

When you judge the people that you perceive, you're not utilizing your empath abilities to the fullest. Judgment lowers your ability to be perceptive. Empaths need to listen with an open mind. Keep your judgments out of the picture because empathetic people are not judgmental. For true empathy to take place, you need to forget your point of view and put yourself in their shoes. When you do this, you may realize that the other person is just reacting to the experience or situation which they may be going through in the only way they know how to. They may not have made the right decision or reacted in the right way, but it was the only way they knew at that time.

*Y*our ability to be perceptive is going to decrease based on the amount of judgment you have. Judgment causes you to measure people, and as soon as you engage in such an activity, you're falling out of tune with your intuition about others. To become a more empathic person, you're going to need to adopt a neutral attitude and avoid being too opinionated.

For example, if you're who is judgmental and opinionated by nature, you're going to have to tone it down significantly if you want to improve your social skills. Strengthening your powers of empathy is about trying to understand the other person; it isn't about you. How do you minimize the judgment? By allowing people to be in the space of life, they are currently in and respect that for what it is. We naturally see things from our point of view first before anyone else's. Instead of trying to look at a situation through the eyes of another, we prefer to convince them why they should see things from our point of view instead. Instead of accepting their ideas and opinions, reject them if it is not something we want to hear. We have all been guilty of this, no question about it.

*O*nly once you let go of your judgment and work on strengthening your empathic abilities can your relationships start to change. The world would get along much better if we could all learn to respect each other's differences. Conflicts would be minimized if we learned to exercise understanding rather than judgment. If we stopped to consider other people's point of view more, social interactions would be very different indeed.

*S*tep 2: Don't Take It Personally

It's easy to feel like it's about you or confuse the emotions and feelings you're getting from others as something that is coming from you. If you do perceive someone's thoughts and emotions, and they happen to be about you, try to avoid taking it personally right from the start. This is *information*. When you take it personally, you're blocking your mind from being open and receptive. You're shutting out the powers of intuition that should get your senses tingling because your mind is defensive and rejecting the information that is coming your way.

*S*tep 3: Create Dialogue

Another way to become stronger as an empath and make the best use of your gifts is to create dialogue. When you sense that someone has more to say, but they're holding back for one reason or another, *encourage them* to speak their mind by creating an opportunity to do so. Avoid questions that tend to end with a yes or a no, with no chance of prolonging the conversation. What you're after are open questions. The kind of questions that help you engage deeply with the person shows your interest and encourage the person to keep on talking.

*E*ncouraging dialogue is easy enough when you pay close attention to the details. Not only does it show you've been listening to what they have to say, but they'll also be so delighted that you remember that they, in turn, will remember you as a great conversationalist. Paying attention to detail makes the speaker feel appreciated and valued, and in doing so, you build a much stronger bond and connection which them. Some empaths have already mastered the art of creating dialogue, and they're so in tune and perceptive that they can complete the sentences of their significant other, family member, or sometimes close friends too. Even before the other person has uttered a word.

*S*tep 4: Try Not to "Fix" People

Not everyone needs to be "fixed." Sometimes people just want someone to listen to them. Someone to talk to where they can vent their feelings. Empaths are there to help, but help does not always mean "fix." To be effective as an empath, you need to be able to listen effectively and really pay attention to what someone else has to say. You are the one they will go to when they feel something needs to be improved, and when they feel you are taking their concerns seriously, no matter how small it may be, they will feel appreciated. Remember, empaths are not here to "fix." They are here to *guide,* and that's what you should be focusing on energy on if you want to use your gifts in a better way. You're here to support, to understand, to nurture, to let them know that their voice matters and they can be heard.

*A*s an empath, you already have the gift of being more in tune with people than the common person can. But trying to "fix" everyone and everything is a common mistake that gets made by many empaths who have not fully understood their gifts yet. One way to strengthen your gift is to make yourself accessible to the people who need you. Let's imagine for a moment that you are an empath, and you also happen to be in a leadership-type role in your job. Making yourself accessible here means making yourself not just an approachable figure to your team who is willing and ready to listen to their complaints, but to be a successful leader, you need to make yourself open and accessible to receiving criticism too. It takes real courage for a leader to make themselves open to it because no one ever likes listening to negative things about themselves. When having a one-on-one conversation with a member of your team, listen to their voice inflections, the tone of their voice, which words they emphasize on, how do they sound when they are expressing what they feel.

. . .

*T*hese are valuable keys and skills that will enable you to really connect with your team, be emphatic towards them, be compassionate, be understanding, and nurturing in a way that they really need. Don't just listen to what they are saying, but listen to what they are trying to tell you and tune in to them in a way a lot of leaders fail to do today. *Listen* with an open mind and without trying to "fix" the situation right away. Let them pour their heart out to you first and then see what can be done from there.

DEVELOPING EMOTIONAL
INTELLIGENCE

EMOTIONS ARE the breath of life. Our emotions are what make us so wonderfully human. Emotions color our world, and the one who can master their emotions can master actions. When you're aware of your emotions, you're better able to own it, claim it, and overcome it. This includes the emotions of others that you might have to deal with. Empathy is one of the five main components of emotional intelligence. An empath who has mastered emotional intelligence is an empath that is happier and more resilient because they have learned how to *control* emotions in themselves and others instead of letting *emotions control them.* If you have not mastered emotional intelligence, don't worry, it is a skill that can be learned.

For empaths in a leadership position, empathy is a critical component. There are three types of empathy that are essential for effective leadership, and each one of the three has strengths of their own. The empathy and social skills aspect of emotional intelligence means being equipped with the ability to attend to the emotions of others too. By adopting these methods to your communication style and approach, you'll find it easier to manage the way people respond and communicate with you in return. An angry customer, for example, could be appeased when you choose to greet them with a smile and respond in an empathetic manner to their complaints by chatting with them and being as understanding as possible, you'll successfully manage your emotions and theirs without anyone doing or saying something they might regret.

Before we dive deeper into empathy as a key emotional intelligence component, let's talk about what the three types of empathy are:

- **Cognitive Empathy -** This gives you the ability to understand the way people think and to see things clearly from their point of view. This is helpful when it is time to give performance feedback or communication. It gives you the ability to communicate your points across in the way that the other party can understand and a way that makes sense for them.

- **Emotional Empathy -** This is the kind of empathy that resonates strongly with empaths. An empathic leader is someone who considers the emotions of others, and they go the extra mile to use this emotional knowledge to better understand the people they have to look after. Emotional empathy is critical for any kind of job where you need to relate to people. Client management, sales, teamwork and more because it is emotional empathy that creates chemistry between people and enables them to work well together. Emotional empathy creates a sense of rapport and simpatico, and empaths who have mastered this ability will go on to become effective leaders of the groups that they lead.

- **Empathic Concern** - Empaths with empathic concern spontaneously help out anyone whom they see might be struggling or in trouble. Without even thinking twice. Empathic concern is the quality that creates outstanding leaders. These are the leaders who take the time to listen and help their team develop their strengths. These are the leaders who take the time to give corrective feedback.

By now, you've probably determined that you're an empath. But the question you're asking yourself is, *what does empathy have to do with emotional intelligence?*

Understanding Empathy as a Core Emotional Intelligence Skill

We often hear about the need for more empathy in the world, and it's true. You've probably seen what a lack of empathy can do in one way or another. Friends who no longer see eye to eye. Colleagues who can no longer relate to the people they work with. Parents who have forgotten what it was like to be a teenager. Teenagers who can't understand why their parents do what they do (even though it is from a place of good intention and love). Most of us try to get others to understand our feelings and our point of view, *but do we put that same effort into trying to understand others?*

Empathy is the ability to thoughtfully consider the feelings of others, along with other factors in the process of making an intelligent decision. Being an empath, you have the power to manage situations, to make people happy or do the opposite. To calm yourself and others around you. To regulate yourself especially when it matters the most, like in a professional setting for example.

Empathy is part of a bigger concept called emotional intelligence. That's why you often find emotionally intelligent people in the top leadership positions. Humans, by nature, are social creatures (yes, even introverts). Nobody can survive in isolation for long and be completely happy about it. We crave human companionship on a deeper level, which is why we often surround ourselves with others to avoid loneliness. But, being around others and being able to connect with them, are two different things entirely. You could be surrounded by a large group of people at any given time and still feel lonely because you have a hard time making a connection with anyone. Emotional intelligence can essentially be summed up in two ways - the ability to recognize, understand, and manage your own personal emotions, and the ability to influence the emotions of others. In Daniel Goleman's book, *Emotional Intelligence,* he divided emotional intelligence into 5 core principles:

- Self-awareness
- Self-regulation
- Motivation
- Empathy
- Social skills

Empathy helps emotionally intelligent individuals recognize and anticipate the needs of another individual, which is essentially what an empath does naturally. They then use this ability to work on fostering and building powerful relationships with a diverse group of people. Because they have the capacity to identify the needs and wants of another person, they are able to decipher the feelings of others, sometimes even preventing conflict before it happens because they can sense what's brewing underneath the surface. The more you can decipher the feelings of people, the better you can manage the thoughts and approaches you send them. Our emotions make up a large part of who we are. We are emotional, and sometimes we respond according to those emotions. We even make decisions based on those emotions. Having emotional intelligence is just as important to a person's success in life. For an empath, emotional intelligence is a way to find balance and to avoid being so overwhelmed by the emotional experiences you take on each day. Not only will you be able to manage and regulate your own emotions, but you can learn to influence the minds of the people around you too, as you learn to master and become better at.

Empathetic people excel at:

- Recognizing, anticipating and meeting a person's needs
- Developing the needs of other people and bolstering their individual abilities
- Taking advantage of diversity by cultivating opportunities among different people
- Developing political awareness by understanding the current emotional state of people and fostering powerful relationships
- Focusing on identifying feelings and wants of other people

*E*motional intelligence is a learned skill, which means even if you're not an empath, you can still learn how to be an empathetic person by utilizing these practical tips below to increase empathy:

- **Learning to Listen Without Interruption** - This is easier said than done. If you've ever tried listening without saying a word or sharing an opinion you thought was brilliant, you'll know how hard it can be to hold your tongue at times. Listening intently can be a challenge. When we listen, most of us end up listening to give an answer instead of just listening. When you are the listener- do just that. Pay attention to what is being said and to empathize with your speaker.

- **Smiling Sincercly** - You know this, everyone knows this- a smile can light up the darkest days because it is contagious. You smile, they smile, everyone smiles. Thank the cingulate cortex for this amazing facial expression. Smiling releases all the feel-good chemicals from the brain, and it also activates all the happy neurons. It also increases your health and you'll be doing yourself a favor and the people around you just by smiling. It just brightens up everyone's day.

- **Using A Person's Name In the Conversation** - A simple

nod while a person talks in a meeting shows that you are encouraging them and also agreeing to their ideas. This gesture, as simple as it is, makes a great impact on your relationship with your colleagues, team, and even with your boss. What's even better if you use their name along with the encouragement.

- **Empathize Regardless of Differences -** You may not share your beliefs with the people around you and vice versa. When these situations come up, you can approach your conversation with people just by saying simple things like 'That's interesting,' "Wow, I never knew that, tell me more.'

- **Being Present -** Simple gestures is all it takes to be fully present at the conversation or situation that is happening. You can start by putting your phone away, not connecting to any digital device that you have, and not answering calls or checking your email while you interact with someone. A study done by Albert Mehrabian, Professor Emeritus at UCLA, says that only seven percent of what is communicated is accounted for. The other 93 percent is contained in our body language and our tone of voice. If you are not present when someone is speaking, you will definitely miss the bulk of what the other person is saying.

- **Offer Genuine Praise and Recognition -** When giving

recognition towards a colleague or a team member, move beyond just saying *"Well done"* or *"Good job."* Dig a little deeper and give constructive feedback and go along with feedback like *"You did really good research on this difficult topic."*

- **Encourage Deep Conversations -** When you want to empathize with someone, you want to understand a person's point of view or even the challenges they face, and this requires that you move the conversation beyond what the weather is like. This also doesn't mean you are asking them about their personal matters. You can start the conversation by talking about your own personal experiences on a certain topic and see if your colleague is comfortable talking about it. The above suggestions are just some of the ways you can empathize with someone and it is probably the safest and simplest way to jump into a situation that you are not familiar with. Just remember that when you speak to someone, use their name, smile at them and listen without interrupting them. All of this will lay the foundation for better rapport between you and them which will make way for a better relationship and help you in influencing them positively in the future.

The Art of Emotional Control

We don't give enough credit to just how powerful emotions can be. When you learn to control your emotions, you learn to control *your life and your destiny.* Think about it. The vast majority of people act out of impulse, and this is evident in moments of anger. We lash out when we're angry. We make impulsive decisions when we're emotional. We might do or say things in the heat of the emotional moment that we later come to regret. The thing is, no one admits that their reactions were a result of poor emotional control. There is always a reason or a justification as to why they behaved the way they did. But the truth is, poor reactions stem from a lack of emotional control. People let their emotions dictate their decisions and actions, and then look for excuses and reasons to justify their behavior, trying to make it seem okay. But it isn't okay.

Experiencing any emotion in excess is never a good thing, even for empaths. When something is experienced in excess, it makes it that much easier for you to feel overwhelmed and on the brink of losing control. Even excessive amounts of happiness is not a good thing, because that euphoria and happiness can result in you making decisions you normally would not. Too much empathy can be a bad thing too, especially when it starts to affect you more than it should. With empathy, you're trying to experience what the other person is going through, which means if they feel stressed, so do you. If they feel anxious or angry, you feel the same. Depending on your skills, you might even be able to feel their physical pain, not just the emotional pain alone, and if you absorb these emotions into your body and allow them to linger, they could start to emotionally hijack your body and mind. When you're an empath that taking on someone else's emotions, you become susceptible to feeling unhappy or miserable. Handling emotions can be a draining ordeal, and when you have to deal with the emotions of others on top of your own, your energy levels can quickly start to deplete. When left unbridled, empathy could potentially lead to a spike in your cortisol levels, which then makes it more difficult for you to manage your emotions. When you allow other people's emotions to affect you, you start to feel responsible for them, and you want to help them overcome their pain. You start feeling stressed about what you can do to help them feel better. But the thing is, if you try to help them too much, you might come off as intrusive, even if your intentions may be good.

When you control your emotions, you're less likely to let your emotions get the better of you. When you learn the art of emotional control, you're more likely to make a decision based on a rational decision-making process. In other words, you think carefully and weigh the pros and cons instead of reacting instinctively based on what you feel at the time. Emotional control is also crucial because it enables you to respond to others based on your values and character. As an empath, this is going to be of tremendous help in ensuring that you don't get swept up by both your emotions and that of the other person. A lack of emotional management is the reason so many people underperform, even the ones with high IQ. One of the first few things you must do for yourself in your efforts to become more emotionally intelligent is to make a personal commitment. Commit to yourself that from now on, you're no longer going to dwell on past emotional mistakes or failures. Commit to yourself that from now on, you're only going to look forwards, towards improvement. Commit to doing the things you know you must do to become better.

The art of emotional control first starts with your personal commitment to change. You have to want to see change, desire to make that change happen. That's the only way you're going to give this your 100% effort. When you make a commitment to change who you are, you're mentally preparing yourself to take the necessary action needed. You're dedicating f yourself to making this change for the better. If you ever struggled to control your emotions, you're not alone. But what a lot of people don't realize is that we *create* the emotions we feel. We *choose* the way we feel at any given time, empaths included. The art of emotional control then begins with the steps below:

- **Identifying Your Emotions -** Uncertainty about the type of emotion you're experiencing will leave you struggling to generate the appropriate response. Noticing your feelings alone is just one part of the process. Notice the way that they make you feel physically and give them a name so you can identify with them even better. *Friendly, happy, proud, nervous, angry, upset, disappointed.* These are just some of the names you could give the emotions that you're feeling. Put them in a sentence and say, *"This makes me feel proud"* or *"This makes me nervous."* Clearly defining your emotions is how you train yourself to focus on pulling your attention inwards, to where it matters the most.

- **Acknowledge and Appreciate Your Emotion -** Yes, even the negative ones because resisting emotions is not a healthy approach to take. Emotions are a part of who you are, and if you reject them, it's only going to make it harder to control. Resisting emotions causes uncertainty, and it may even stop you from using the emotion to your advantage. For example, something happened that caused you to feel frustrated. Instead of fighting the frustration, try to acknowledge it and the circumstances that made you feel that way.

- **Analyzing the Emotion -** Be curious about your emotions in this stage. Curiosity opens the door to new perspectives and opportunities. It provides unique insight into your emotions and the circumstances you find yourself in. Ask yourself, *"What is the true value of the emotion I'm feeling? In what way does this emotion serve me? What can I do to make things better?"*. Remember, emotions are felt for a reason, so you're probably feeling this emotion for a purpose. Emotions are capable of teaching us valuable lessons about ourselves and our circumstances, so don't be afraid to analyze them.

- **Formulating Multiple Responses -** There is more than one way to approach any emotional situation you face. Think about all the times in the past, where you may not have had the best reaction to certain situations because your judgment was impaired by your emotions. If faced with a similar situation again in the future, how would you handle things differently and why? Practice listing out all the different responses and reactions you would have, and ask yourself if this is what an emotionally intelligent person would do? How well are you regulating your reactions to these challenging emotional situations? You're not dwelling on the past, but rather using these past experiences as lessons which you can learn from. Observing what didn't work in the past so you don't repeat those same mistakes again in the future.

- **Reframe Your Perspective** - Your emotions have a lot to do with the way that you perceive certain situations and events. For example, if you're already feeling nervous and worried, getting an email from your boss saying that they want to see, you might aggravate your emotions even further. You may perceive it as bad news that you're about to be told off for a mistake that you made. Perhaps even fired. You'd probably be envisioning all the worst possible scenarios. Now, if you were to receive that same email from your boss but you were feeling happy or jubilant that day, you'd perceive the situation in an entirely different light. You might think that your boss wants to discuss a new opportunity, or give you some great feedback. Maybe even promote you. This is the perfect example to illustrate just how big of an influence our emotions can have on the way that we perceive things, and why it is important to start focusing on what's going on internally within you. Being able to identify your emotions makes it easier to reframe your thoughts by viewing situations from a realistic perspective.

How to Master Your Emotions

Let's look at the story of two different men named John and Jim. Two different individuals with different world views, two different goals, and two different paths in life.

John believes there are two kinds of people in the world. These are the conquerors and the ones who are conquered. To become someone great in the world, you need to be a conqueror. It's a harsh world out there, and you need to be bold and determined if you want to survive and succeed. You need to determine who is going to conquer the world with you. As a child, John read a lot and he loved stories of Greek heroes who displayed virtues like bravery and courage. He admired them because they were not followers. They were strong, powerful leaders, which were qualities he looked up to. John had to work hard from a young age for everything that he had because his family was not wealthy. This upbringing led John to believe that a person is responsible for the actions they take that shape the course of their life. One day, John encountered a homeless man who asked him if he had any change to spare. John realized that he was looking at a man who was conquered in life. John begins to wonder how this man had allowed himself to be conquered to this point. How many mistakes did the man make for him to end up where he is right now. Why is this man not taking responsibility for his life to change it or dig himself out of the hole? John believed this man was not trying hard enough and chose instead to take the easy way out by seeking help from those who had to work hard for everything they have. John believed if the man wanted to fish, then he had to be taught how to fish instead of having fish handed to him. John became annoyed by what he perceived to be the man's weakness and refused to give him a single penny. John believed that giving in to what the homeless man wanted would only enable his destructive attitude and poor lifestyle habits.

Jim believes there are two kinds of people in this world. The first are the people who can help, and the second is the people who need help. Growing up, Jim's father taught him that the highest good was when you served those who have nothing and to do what you can to lift them up. Life is full of hard knocks and challenges, and those who were in a position to help should lend a helping hand. Jim read a lot as a child, and the stories he was drawn to the most were those of spiritual leaders who dedicated their lives to helping others. Jim came from a wealthy family and felt indebted to help those who were not as fortunate and blessed as he was. One day, Jim came across a homeless man who asked him for some change. Jim knew he was looking at a man who was all alone and abandoned by society. A man who had no one else to turn to, no roof over his head, and no inkling of where his next meal was coming from. Jim felt like crying when he thought of this man's plight. Jim took out the money he had in his pocket and gave it to the man.

Both John and Jim have very unique world views that are shaped by their past experiences. Both perceived the homeless man in a very different way. Where John saw someone who was weak, Jim saw someone who was forsaken and in need of help. Their emotions were heavily impacted by what they thought they were seeing. The truth was, both men had no idea of the circumstances that led the homeless man to this position. This same thing can be said in real life. From a young age, all of us are surrounded by an invisible force that is subtly shaping our perspectives and world views. This force is our environment and our culture, and the knowledge that we grab from this structure is what enables us to navigate the world. In John's world, for example, anger was a tool he used to help him grow stronger while Jim used compassion that led him to empathize strongly with others and become a giver. What if John and Jim had their roles reversed? What if their lives were reversed? Would they perceive the world differently? Would they feel any differently about the homeless man?

The master of emotions is the one who can change their perspectives and see the world around them differently, despite being brought up in a certain way by the invisible force. The ability to change the invisible force allows you to gather a diverse set of concepts so you can view one scenario from multiple perspectives. When you learn to master your emotions, you're not John or Jim. You become *both,* or you can be either one depending on your circumstances. Emotional mastery is about understanding perspectives from various angles. The better you understand your emotions and the emotions of people around, the more apt you will be at deciphering the way they feel and how you should respond to that. Conflicts, hurt feelings, and misunderstandings are minimized when you develop the ability to see things from someone else's point of view. When a friend has had a particularly rough week at work, and they happen to be short-tempered or snappish when you try to engage them in a conversation, emotional mastery is the skill that is going to give you the ability you need to put things into perspective. Instead of feeling hurt, possibly even angry with your friend for what they did, you'll be able to reflect on why they reacted that way and understand where they're coming from. Empathy is an important yet underrated skill, and it can make such a difference in the way you communicate once you know how to use it.

You experience dozens (if not hundreds) of emotions on a daily basis. Each emotion combines personality, context, and experience to create a mental state that is unique to you as an individual. Despite the emotional diversity possibilities, most of us group our emotions into a few simple categories that make it easy for us to understand. For example, you might say, *"I feel bad"* to describe nearly every negative emotion (don't forget you're supposed to specifically put a name to each emotion you feel). Being an empath, it is important you learn to master your emotions to avoid emotions getting the best of you, especially when you feel so much more of it than others do.

- **Focus on What Makes You Happy** - Learning to master your emotions is not just about getting it under control; it is about reconnecting with yourself too, and finding your happiness once more. The best way to do that is to do something that makes you happy. When you find yourself in an emotional situation and you're struggling to get a hold of yourself, walk away and choose instead to do something that makes you happy. As hard as it may be to ignore the compelling urge to help others, you can't help anyone if you're not in control of yourself. Each time you actively try to engage in an activity that brings you joy, you'll find your negative emotions ebbing away quicker with each effort you make. Harness the all-consuming power of happiness, because it's a good kind of emotion which will benefit you and everyone else around you. A happier state of mind also makes it much easier for you to think with clarity, and in doing so, gives you a much better handle at controlling your emotions.

- **Avoid Focusing on Your Worries -** Nothing good will ever come out of worrying. There's always going to be a reason to worry, but why worry about what you cannot change? Emotionally intelligent people don't do that. They know that worrying does nothing except waste your precious time, which could instead be spent devising strategies to help you get to the next phase of your mission to master your emotions. Successful people are mentally tough because they do not waste their energy on what is beyond their control. Instead, they shift their focus toward what needs to be done. If it works, it works; if it doesn't they find a way to make it work the next time they attempt it.

- **Pay More Attention To the Good** - Writing down your positive experiences can have a significant impact on your mood. It's easier to focus on what negative episodes may be taking place in our lives. If we go through the entire day experiencing 10 positive episodes and one negative episode, the negative episode is the one that is going to resonate the strongest. It's how our mind works. To make it easier to pay more attention to positive experiences, it helps to write it down, so there's something for you to refer to when you need it.

- **Maintain Realistic Expectations** - This is an important one for empaths in particular because as much as you want to change the world, there's only so much you can do, and you need to be realistic about your capabilities. If you don't, your emotions are always going to get the best of you when you can't help someone despite trying your very best. Unrealistic expectations will only kill your happiness. Learning how to master your emotions is something that is going to happen over time. You are essentially cultivating a better version of yourself. Building anything from scratch is always going to take time, but those who have been patient enough remain optimistic and happy throughout the process because they know that good things always take time.

EMPATH ON THE JOB

IF YOU'RE an empath and highly sensitive, the kind of career you want to get involved in are the ones that connect you with emotions of joy. Being an empath is hard work as it is, and if you're in a profession that is draining you because there's such a high level of negativity and unhappiness you encounter on the job, that's not going to be good for your wellbeing. Empaths are driven to help people and a career that focuses on that passion for helping others.

The Best Career for Empaths

It is important for everyone to feel at peace and at least somewhat happy in their place of work. For an empath, this is even more of a necessity because of your highly sensitive nature. You may love what you do, but if there is too much in the job that is causing you to burn out, eventually, you're going to have to leave that job when you can no longer cope. Empaths have a lot of qualities that can be extremely beneficial in the workplace. For example:

- Empaths are loyal and dedicated
- Empaths are wonderful listeners
- Empaths are very detail-oriented
- Empaths are organized and fair
- Empaths are independent, and they don't require a lot of supervision
- Empaths are sensitive to the needs and emotions of others, which makes them great team players.

Are there certain kinds of jobs that an empath should avoid? Yes, there is. One of them being jobs that are sales focused and jobs that include a lot of confrontation. Jobs, where you're required to deal with people non-stop for several hours a day, is exhausting for an empath to handle. Cut-throat and competitive jobs are also not suited for empaths because it is simply not in their nature to betray or backstab another for their own personal gain. Any jobs that take place in a loud, hectic environment are the kind of jobs empaths should endeavor to stay away from.

Of course, not all work environments are the same. One empath might have an entirely different experience from another depending on the environment they find themselves in. Every empath is different, and the kind of job you would enjoy the most would be based on your principles, values, and what your interest or calling is. Here are some examples of the types of careers that might suit you best if you're an empath:

- **Counselor or Therapist** - This is probably one of the few jobs in which an empath can really thrive. It fulfills the calling of wanting to make a difference in the lives of others, you'll excel at this job because you're naturally a great listener, there are no crowd and no large groups of people at a time to deal with, and you get to focus on your goal of helping the person under your care.

- **Nurses** - Empaths are natural caregivers and healers, which makes them perfect for this job. Being a nurse allows you to put your natural empathic gifts to good use, helping patients stay calm when they feel unsettled and in pain. You're literally the support system for the patients who need it. The demand for quality nurses is never going to diminish, which means you'll always be assured of a job since nursing is an essential healthcare service.

- **Psychologists** - You're the nurse and the healer of the mental world for those who need someone to talk to about their mental health issues. Mental health is just as much of a concern these days as physical health, and these issues can be equally debilitating if not properly attended to. Since empaths have an innate talent for understanding emotions and the ability to listen actively, this makes them perfect for this job since they can have a soothing and calming effect on the people they talk to.
- **Veterinarians** - Empaths with the ability to connect with animals will love working in this role. Some empaths are even able to form such a strong bond and connection with

the animals that they have been referred to as "animal whisperers." An empath in this role has the ability to both calm and soothe the animals in their care as well as the frantic owners who might be worried about their pets. It gives the owners a little more peace of mind knowing their beloved pets are in good hands.

- **Graphic Designer** - The possible pros of this job is how it taps into your creative nature. It lets you explore your creative and imaginative side, and although you do come into contact with people, for the most part, you get to work independently and sometimes in a team. This minimizes the chances of you being emotionally drained on the job.

- **Accountant** - Being an accountant lets you tap into your analytical, problem-solving side if that is what you enjoy best from your empathic abilities. If solving problems makes you happy, this job might be something you enjoy.

- **Life Coach** - An empath's natural desire to want to help people better their lives is one reason why they will love their job as a life coach. Working one on one with your clients, you will help them be the best version of themselves that they can be. You'll always have their best interest at heart because it is in your nature. Encouraging others to meet their goals is one of the most fulfilling things that you can do.

- **Online Business Owner -** The advantage of this job is the minimal face to face interaction with your customers, which means minimal energy drain. There's also the independence and flexible hours that come with the job, which gives you the freedom to recharge and find your balance again when you feel the need for it.

- **Private Tutor -** If you love teaching but being in a room full of students is a strain on your emotions because of your empathic nature, the next best option would be to consider private tutoring. You still get to do what you love, helping, and teaching others, but dealing with one student at a time is not going to be as stressful and gives you a sense of control. You set your hours and in between, you get time to yourself to recuperate if needed.

- **Actor -** The ability to feel the emotions of others and to feel it so deeply that it becomes a part of you is what makes empaths such great actors. However, this job might not be for every empath because being an actor can put an immense strain on an empath's emotional state. Especially when they have to juggle multiple emotions all at once.

How to Thrive At Work

Empaths need to find ways to thrive at work without getting overwhelmed and drained. Being affected by emotions can be a real liability on the job, especially if it gets to a stage where it is impacting your ability to perform. Without the proper coping techniques to handle themselves, an empath can easily find themselves stressed and overwhelmed at the workplace, especially if you happen to be working with a lot of negative and toxic personalities. Here is how you make the most of your empathic nature and thrive at work without feeling drained or weighed down too heavily by the emotions of others:

- **Spend More Time Doing and Less Time Overthinking -** It's best to keep yourself busy when you're on the job. If you're always occupied handling one task after another, you don't have as much free time to dwell on emotions because you've got deadlines to meet. Since an empath tends to feel emotions so strongly, they're also prone to overthinking, trying to analyze what it all means.
- **Avoid Taking Everything Personally -** It's hard to feel like it's not about you when you feel emotions so intensely, but yes, not everything is a personal attack against you. That is why it's important to learn how to identify emotions using emotional intelligence, so you can figure out which emotions are yours and separate yourself from confusing the emotions of others as things that you are feeling. Taking everything personally can result in a "me-against-the-world" thinking, which can be very lonely and isolating if you feel like no one understands you, and everything is a personal attack against you.

- **Learning to Let Things Go** - Empaths are individuals who easily feel overwhelmed because of how much they are taking on from other people. Once you learn to differentiate between the emotions that are yours and those that belong to someone else, it's time to let go of the emotions that aren't yours. You would also need to learn to let go of the guilt of not being able to help everyone. If you've tried your best, that's all you can hope for. After all, your capacity as a human being is limited. Push yourself too hard, and you'll only end up overwhelmed and exhausted, unable to help anyone.

- **Make Time to Be Alone** - Break times can also be alone times. Gather your thoughts and compose yourself by stepping away from everyone at work when it is your designated break time so you can spend some time alone quietly. During those few minutes alone, if it helps and the space permits, try meditating, visualization, or going for a quick walk in nature. Whatever you need to feel better so you can come back to work somewhat refreshed and ready to tackle the next half of the job until it's time for a break again.

- **Be Around Positive-Minded People** - Not all colleagues are alike. There are bound to be at least one, two, or several people at work who are positive-minded and, if you can, seek them out and actively spend time in their company. Surrounding yourself with positive people is the key for anyone to thrive and succeed in this world, not just empaths. You can learn a lot from these individuals and more importantly, they infuse you with the positive energy you need to feel better.

- **Be Clear About What Your Needs Are and Prioritize Them** - In rare cases, you might need to set aside your own needs to prioritize others. For example, if you were working as a counselor or a healer where your clients truly need your help. Where possible, avoid sacrificing your needs too much for the sake of others. Neglecting your own needs is the quickest way to burn out. To thrive at work, you need to make a list of what your needs and priorities are. Keep that list with you on your desk at work to remind yourself that you need to make yourself a priority or risk burning out.

Protecting Yourself from Toxic People

Empaths are caring, compassionate, helpful, gentle, and nurturing. Because they are driven by such a strong desire to help, an empath is unlikely to immediately dismiss someone without valid cause. Unfortunately, this makes them easily susceptible to falling into unhealthy relationships with the wrong type of individuals. An empath can quickly become drained in the wrong type of environment surrounded by the wrong people, especially if they're around toxic people. Empaths are loyal and loving to a fault sometimes, and because of their nature, they want to see the good in everyone, even in toxic personalities.

Who are these toxic personalities? Narcissists, for one. Throughout our lifetime, we will engage in many relationships. Friendships that bring us joy, romantic relationships which are exhilarating and family relationships which can be supportive. Unfortunately, these relationships could also be destructive, which is usually the moment it becomes toxic. The kind of people that you surround yourself with can be one of two things: they can either be your greatest blessing, or they can be the negative force that drags you down. People get into unhealthy and destructive relationships all the time, that is not uncommon. For an empath though, this experience is going to be 10 times worse than it is for everyone else because of how sensitive they are to emotions. Emotional abuse is the worse thing that can happen to an empath. The union between an empath and a narcissist is a terrible idea. These two personalities are like two parallel lines that never get to meet. It is so important as an empath that you assess the kind of people you allow into your life. What kind of influence do they have over you? Are they inspiring you? Or are they draining you?

A narcissist will perceive an empath as an easy victim, someone who is weak because of their kind and benevolent nature. If the empath does not have a level of control over their emotions, they will end up becoming emotional sponges when a narcissist comes into the picture, absorbing the wrong energies of the exploitive and toxic personality. The reason why empaths and narcissists should never be together is that empaths are out there to heal the world and make it a better place, and they can't stand to see anyone in pain. A narcissist, however, is the kind of personality that capitalizes on someone else's misery. Why do these toxic individuals have such a powerful impact on our lives? Because they leech on your emotions. Being constantly surrounded by people who criticize you, complain and affect you both emotionally and physically is an exhausting affair. Negativity is a powerful force, and being around these individuals too much might make you tempted to get sucked into their cycle of misery. The narcissist is not someone who needs healing. They are someone who is there to exploit the goodness of others. They get into relationships with empaths and then manipulate, belittle, and use them. A toxic relationship is one that can be very damaging because of how it can chip away at your confidence. Being around the constant negativity which toxic people emit will eventually undermine your dignity, affect your self-esteem and perhaps even warp your personality depending on the relationship's impact.

Narcissists are among the most dangerous types of toxic personalities because they have exaggerated levels of self-esteem. They believe they are the picture of perfection, and to themselves, they are infallible. Depending on the individual in question, the strength of the narcissistic tendencies would vary in strength, with some people having a stronger disposition towards this personality than others. Narcissism is associated with grandiosity, a distinct lack of empathy, egotism, and pride. Confront a narcissist about their behavior and you'll immediately be met with denial. Yes, even if you were to present them with evidence about their narcissistic tendencies, they'll deny it point-blank and refuse to accept the truth, even if it is literally staring them in the face. Believe it or not, this is actually one way they continue to whole their victims captive, by denying any kind of wrongdoing and not owning up to their mistakes. They'll deny is so often that the victim will begin to question if they were the ones who were in the wrong after all. That perhaps they misjudged the narcissist. Bear in mind that the narcissist is a master manipulator, and they will gaslight their victims so much that the victims give in and be inclined to believe what the narcissist is telling them after all.

The side effects which result from the toxic relationship can either happen immediately or over time. In an empath's case, it can happen almost immediately. Narcissists crave attention. They need it to feed into their egos and belief about their own self-importance. If they can't get it from you through admiration, they will resort to another approach by getting you to feel sorry for them instead. They shift the focus of your attention towards them, their needs, and their so-called "misfortunes." They'll regale you with tales that make you feel sorry for them, and feel bad enough for them to shower all your time and attention is completely devoted to making them "feel better." They will go to any lengths to get the attention they seek, even if they must make up some stories along the way. Regardless, the consequential distress can leave an impact that will last a lifetime, especially if the wound is something that is difficult to heal. When an empath loves a narcissist, this is what happens:

- **It Starts Out Beautifully** - Almost all relationships start out wonderful during the honeymoon phase, and it's no different when an empath first begins a relationship with a narcissist. However, it won't take long before that quickly fades away into thin air. The common themes which occur in a toxic relationship are generally abuse, which can either be physical or emotional, and the other is co-dependency. Co-dependency is considered an unhealthy and toxic relationship because it starts off involving two people who were already not secure to begin with. These two people then seek each other out and form a relationship, trying to make themselves whole. They don't come into the relationship as independent and self-sufficient individuals.

In this relationship dynamic, the empath will find it hard to accept the changes in their partner because the empath loves so completely and wholeheartedly. They believed with all their heart in the beginning that their partner was the same. One of the reasons why this relationship will start off so beautifully is that the empath naturally shows a lot of love right from the beginning, and they shower the narcissist with all the love and energy they have to give. This is exactly what the narcissist wants, and they will keep taking and taking until there is nothing left to give. Sure, the narcissist will put in some effort in the beginning (as everyone does with all new relationships), and once the empath is convinced they are being loved in return, that is when the tables start to turn. The narcissist will always capitalize on the naivety of the empath.

- **The Narcissist Is The One In Control** - The relationship with a toxic personality will never be one that is fair and balanced. It will always be one-sided, and in this case, the narcissist is the one who is going to be calling all the shots. By nature, the narcissist wants to have control over everyone in their lives, and the empath is in very real danger of losing themselves in the relationship. When you lose yourself in a toxic relationship, your judgment becomes clouded and it is harder to see what is best for yourself anymore. You forget who you are and what you want, and your happiness no longer becomes a priority. You start to get comfortable with it and make excuses for being in that toxic relationship because it feels better than having to deal with the pain of letting go of the person that you love or think you love. The narcissist will want the empath to be dependent on them for everything, and the narcissists try to make the empaths feel like they are fortunate to have them in their lives. That there is no one else out there who will love the empath quite like they can. It is easy to get consumed in a toxic relationship because those types of individuals are so overbearing. When people lose themselves in their relationships, they are no longer themselves anymore and everything becomes all about their partners. The empath is in danger of being loyal and submissive to a fault, feeling guilty at having to cut ties with someone they believe "loves them," even though there can never be any real love when a narcissist is involved.

- **Regular Conflicts** - A loving and gentle soul like the empath is going to eventually feel tired and fatigued when it keeps getting hurt. The narcissist will see an empath as someone they can walk all over because of how loving and accomodating they can be. But empaths are anything but pushovers. They have feelings too, and when they feel their partner is not meeting their needs, agitation and frustration tend to follow. You should never be willing to put up with a toxic relationship. It could end up hurting more than just your feelings. Relationships can be complicated. When it's good, it can be really great. But when it's bad, it could potentially impact your health physically and emotionally. Arguments, confrontation, and conflict are all things that drain an empath considerably, and being trapped in this kind of unhealthy dynamic is going to take its toll on the empath eventually.

- **Your Confidence Suffers A Blow** - Toxic relationships will erode your confidence slowly but surely. This is because you are constantly surrounded by a partner who makes you feel like you are never good enough. They make you feel bad about yourself, casting doubt on your abilities, and even make you question whether you are good enough. Being around this all the time will cause wear and tear on your confidence, stripping you of it until eventually, your self-esteem takes a nosedive. There is only so much an empath can handle before they finally cave under the constant pressure and emotional turmoil of being made to feel like they are never good enough no matter what they do. Nothing is a bigger energy drainer than spending all of your efforts making sure the other person is happy but not receiving the same kind of support in return. When you spend your time around toxic people, it is always "all about them," and you become secondary.

- **When the Relationship Ends, the Empath Feels Guilty** - Empaths are naturally kind, and they will try to make up for things that are not their fault sometimes. When in a relationship with this type of toxic behavior, you will often be made to feel "guilty" even when there is no reason for you to feel bad. This type of toxic relationship can occur amongst friends, co-workers, families, and couples. The toxic person will try to control and manipulate the situation to their benefit by inducing guilt upon you, sometimes subtly disguised. For example, the narcissist would appear to "support" your decision, but then subtly remind you of the things that you're neglecting to make you feel bad. Being around somebody who is toxic for too long will make you feel bad about yourself, insecure, drained, stressed, pressured and even emotionally scarred. Even though the breakup was for the best, the narcissist will have no problem throwing in words that makes the empath feel guilty and selfish for thinking about their own needs.

*N*arcissists are the complete opposite of empaths, that much is clear. These types of individuals are a bit tricky because they can be difficult to spot in the beginning, and they hide their true personalities so well. Narcissists tend to be manipulative and they will always push your buttons and subtly emotionally blackmail you until they get things done their way. They have an ulterior motive and will not hesitate to use information against you if it means they get what they want. Once the relationship is no longer beneficial to the manipulators, they have no qualms about discarding you without a second thought. Yet another reason why the relationship between an empath and a narcissist is so harmful is that the narcissist genuinely believes that the empath owes them a lot, and these are some examples of what these narcissists feel entitled to (even though you don't owe them anything):

- **They Believe You Owe Them Attention** - Narcissists are completely ignorant and oblivious to everyone else's feelings. All they ever think about is themselves, and if you don't give them the attention they think they deserve, they begin emotionally lashing out at you and

making you feel like you're the worst partner in the
world.

- **They Believe They Can Do Anything They Want** - A
  narcissist will have no problem violating your boundaries.
  There is no such thing as respecting boundaries in the eyes
  of the narcissist, simply because they don't care about
  anyone else except themselves. They enjoy pushing others
  to the limits, and they will go to any lengths to do it,
  including pushing past your boundaries or violating rules
  to do so. They may resort to behavior, which includes
  intruding on your personal space, taking or borrowing your
  things without returning them, taking someone else's work
  and passing it off as their own, breaking promises,
  appointments, and even negating on agreements that were
  made. In some extreme cases where you might be
  romantically involved with a narcissistic manipulator, they
  could even resort to tactics that include sexual abuse or
  harassment, domestic violence or abuse, and even verbal
  and emotional abuse. The worst part of it all is some
  narcissists even take pride in their behavior under the
  misguided notion of feeling "powerful" when they see
  someone else suffer at their hands.

- **They Believe You Owe Them Your Loyalty** - They lead
  you to believe that you have a "special connection," and
  thus, the two of you were meant to be together forever.
  They could deceive you into believing that you're special by
  using phrases such as *I've never loved anyone the way that I love*

you, or *I never knew what love was until I met you*. This statement may be true for some people, but it rarely ever holds any truth if you're dealing with a narcissist. It is simply another tactic which they use to reel you in before inflicting even more emotional abuse on you later once you have been lulled into a false sense of security and lead you to believe you owe them your loyalty because they deign to be with you.

ou need to protect yourself from these toxic personalities. You need to protect your energy and your emotions, and you have every right to do it without having to feel bad or selfish. Everyone (empath or not) should protect themselves from overbearingly toxic personalities. It is the only way to reclaim your life and your happiness again and put a stop to these energy vampires. These are several ways an empath can protect themselves from being hurt by the toxic relationships they encounter, and these measures include:

- **Decide What You Want** - Before taking any kind of action, you need to determine what you want from the relationship. No one else can do this step for you because unless they are an empath, they won't be able to fully comprehend what you're going through. You already know that you might not be able to change someone with a toxic personality, so you need to now ask yourself what can you take away from the relationship that you will be okay with. If you decide that you don't want a relationship with them at all, then that is okay too. If the relationship has no hope of changing, then there is only one thing left to do. Plan your exit strategy. Leading up to it, you need to start setting boundaries with your partner, be firm and decisive. They may push back and retaliate because toxic people always want to be in control of the situation, but you need to be just as firm and say no. Stand your ground and do not give in to their demands any longer.

- **Creating A Safe Emotional Space for Yourself -** One method of coping with toxic relationships is to create a space for your emotions. A place where you feel safe enough to express yourself without fear of being judged or ridiculed. You may not be able to find this in the home environment, but there are other outlets that you can utilize to help you find that safe space you need. You could journal about the way you feel and what you're going through, or maybe even blog about it. As long as you have something to release your pent up frustrations. Keeping your feelings bottled up deep inside is never a good move, and it can often lead to depression and feelings of loneliness and isolation.

- **Create A Support System for Yourself -** The support system can be in the form of friends or even other family members that you trust and can confide in. It can even be a counselor or a co-worker that you trust enough to talk to. Reach out to someone and find a support system because you're going to need it to help you through the process of cutting ties with a toxic relationship. It will help a lot in managing your emotions and the stress of dealing with what you may be going through until you feel better.

- **Set Boundaries for the Relationships That You Build -** With any future relationships that you encounter, you should set boundaries to avoid getting hurt again. Set boundaries for what you're willing to put up with and stick to it as best you can. Keeping and maintaining your distance is one of the best things you could do for yourself when it comes to coping with toxic relationships. The more space you put between you and them, the better you will feel. If you can't avoid these personalities entirely (for example, if the narcissist is not a romantic partner but a friend or family member), then keep the contact with them to a minimum. Find ways to keep yourself busy and always have something to do so you have an excuse not to be around them.

SURVIVING YOUR GIFT

As wonderful as it can be to be an empath, it is also a tough gift to have. Not everyone is going to understand your abilities, some may mock you because they don't believe in it, and there will be many times in your life when you wish you did not have this ability at all. There are times when an empath can't help feeling overwhelmed because emotions can be such a powerful force to be reckoned with. It takes great inner strength and emotional intelligence to truly be in control of yourself and the way you feel every step of the way. If you let it, emotions will flood your mind and your being like a tidal wave, especially when you're not equipped with the necessary skills and techniques needed to survive your gift. This final chapter is going to focus on how to keep your gift under control while protecting yourself from getting overwhelmed and exhausted.

Why a Lot of People Can't Handle It

Like anyone else, an empath wants to love and to be loved in return. Although empaths tend to give their all without expecting anything in return, they're only human too. Of course, they would love to be treated with the same love and care that they shower upon other people. One common misconception is that empaths tend to struggle in life because they are *too sensitive* to the energy and emotions around them. But some people actually find it difficult to be around an empath, believe it not. Yes, the empath is not the only one who struggles with their gift. Other people do too. Maybe it's because of the empaths intensity and the way they feel emotions so deeply. A lot of people can't understand or process that because they're *sympathetic*, but not *empathetic*. Both the empath and the people around might also struggle with a fear of intimacy. An empath's friends, family, and even partners may be uncomfortable with the idea of knowing someone can sense the way they feel and what they might be thinking all the time, even if they haven't said a word about it themselves.

Here are some of the reasons why empaths and a lot of people close to them struggle with and find it difficult to handle this gift:

- **Difficulty Forming A Serious Relationship** - Some empaths might be afraid of getting into a serious relationship for fear of being hurt again. For the empath, there's a very good chance they have been through many failed and toxic relationships over the course of their life (and will continue to do so unless they start implementing measures to protect themselves). Eventually, the empaths will reach a point where they are afraid of getting involved in yet another serious relationship and risk getting their hearts broken again. For the one who is on the other side of the relationship with an empath, this wall that the empath puts up in an attempt to protect themselves might make it difficult to form a bond of intimacy. The empath's partner is always going to feel like the empath is holding back a part of themselves, and that might cause frustration and misunderstanding. It may take time before the empath is ready to open their heart again. Unfortunately, some partners either can't understand or are not willing to wait around for things to change.

- **Too Many Questions** - Because of the empath's desire to get to the root of the problem and to try and help others, they prone to asking a lot of questions. They can't help it since they feel everything more intensely than other people do. To them, everything has a deeper meaning. Sometimes they don't accept things at face value if they sense there might be more going on, but despite their genuine desire to help, some people might find this uncomfortable as they think the empath might be coming on too strong. Not everyone feels comfortable with being asked too many questions, especially in the initial stages of a relationship, and an empath's desire to help might end up backfiring on them.

- **Too Many Expectations About Honesty** - Most empaths are genuine, and their actions, motives, and intentions usually stem from a good place. The downside is, this expectation of honesty that they project onto others might be the cause of a lot of disappointment, especially in a romantic relationship. Part of an empath's ability is to be able to sense when someone is lying to them, and they will call you out on it. Not everyone is comfortable or necessarily happy with this approach. Even if a partner may be lying or holding back to protect the empath's feelings, it can cause a lot of friction (and possibly arguments) if an empath keeps pressing for honesty. That's why not everyone is able to handle being around an empath and why empath's themselves struggle with some of the relationships that they have.

- **They Sense Things Even Before You've Told Them -** Everyone is bound to encounter problems. Personal, professional, or relationship-wise. While most people do want to talk about it at some point, they might not want to do so right away. If they are in a relationship with an empath, the empath might immediately start asking what's wrong if they sense any kind of unhappiness. The empath might not know the actual problem, but they will be able to feel like you're hiding something from them. They'll keep pushing and pressing for an answer because it bothers them when something is wrong. Unfortunately, not everyone is going to be responsive right away, and the more you push them, the further they retreat from you emotionally.

- **Empaths Have Seen the Good and Bad -** Empaths have seen it all. They've seen the beauty in people, and they've also seen the bad in people. With the emotional roller coaster that some relationships put them through, empaths will eventually reach a point when they realize some people are just not going to change (these would be the toxic personalities). No matter how much the empath may want to help, they can't do much if the person themselves refuses to change. It can be a very disappointing moment for an empath when they come to this realization, and they may find it difficult to accept, perhaps even difficult to handle. The empath could end up carrying that guilt around with them for a long time, even though it isn't their fault.

- **Empaths Might Freak Some People Out** - Some people might get freaked out by the idea of what an empath is capable of. Not everyone likes their secrets revealed, and the idea that an empath knows things even though you've tried to hide it and never said anything about it can be extremely uncomfortable for some people. Empaths are also prone to expressing their thoughts and feelings a lot sooner than some people might be comfortable with. Especially when most people don't even know how to process or understand their own feelings. It can be a challenging thing, being around an empath. This whole experience might be a bit too much for some people to handle, and they avoid being around empaths because of it, much to the empath's hurt and dismay.

- **The Mood Swings** - For those who don't understand what it's like to be an empath, they might not be able to comprehend why empaths can swing from one extreme mood to another. Empaths could be happy one moment and then become extremely sad the next. Since an empath feels every emotion 10 times more intensely, it is only natural that the way they express these emotions or the mood swings they experience may be heightened as well. An empath who is struggling to get a handle on their emotions might inadvertently lash out at the people who are closest to them. Some people find this extremely difficult to be around since there's no telling when the empath's mood is going to shift or change just like that.

The Habits of Highly Empathic People

Empaths are a gift to the world around them. No one else will be able to come close to displaying the paragon of goodness and self-lessness the way an empath can if they don't have this ability. Empaths are unique people with equally unique habits. They're not the kind of people you meet every day. Empaths are as rare as their abilities. Anyone can show empathy, which makes spotting a genuine empath a real challenge. Once you are around an empath, you'll start to notice that they have certain quirks and habits about them. These are not habits or quirks you'll see often either. Here are some of the habits of highly empathic people:

- **Cultivating Curiosity** - Most empaths are extremely curious about the people around them. You might say their curiosity is almost insatiable, and they find other people a lot more interesting than themselves. They have no problems striking up a conversation with strangers, and it is their avid curiosity that makes others open up to them too. People want to be heard and they want someone to listen to them, and when an empath comes along with a genuine curiosity about how they are and what they do, it's hard not to warm up to them.

- **They're Good At Making Conversation** - Their natural curiosity enables them to be good conversationalists. They pay attention to what is being said, and this allows them to ask all the right questions to keep the conversation going. To encourage others to open up about their lives, empaths like to focus on open-ended questions and when the other person speaks, the empaths immerse themselves in the moment and listen without interruption. They make a real effort to be present and minimize distractions that take place during a conversation so they can give the other person their full, undivided attention.

- **They Seek Commonalities** - While most people let differences and prejudices be the wall that divides them others, empaths seek out the commonalities they can use to build a bond with others. Empaths focus on what they have in common with others rather than the differences. It is one of the ways they are able to see things from another's perspective because they focus on what they have in common rather than how different their lives or opinions may be. They immerse themselves in the lives of another, join in experiences, volunteer, travel to other countries to experience different cultures, all of which help to broaden their perspective on life.

- **They Tend to Avoid Being In A Crowd -** It's not because they are antisocial, but rather it is because they feel so overwhelmed by all the energy that is coming their way. Crowded environments will with both positive and negative emotions are not a comfortable environment for them, and they would rather avoid it if they can. Some extroverts might find this retreating habit of theirs difficult to understand.

- **They Put Other People's Needs Before Their Own -** Not necessarily the best habit to have since it puts the empath at risk of neglecting themselves (which admittedly tends to happen a lot). Friends, family, and partners of the empath might find this habit frustrating to deal with, especially when they see how emotionally exhausted the empath becomes from constantly placing the needs of others before their own. They spend far too much time being busy helping others and not enough time helping themselves.

- **The Attract People Who Want Their Help Rather Than Their Love -** Loving to a fault is both a blessing and a curse for the empath. Empaths have the habit of giving away too much of themselves and not getting enough love and care in return. Some people are more interested in what the empath can do for them rather than the love they can receive from them, which is one of the many reasons why empaths tend to fall into the trap of associating themselves with toxic individuals.

- **It's Hard to Say "No"** - This happens a lot to an empath. They *know* that they should be saying "no," but it's easier said than done when they sense someone in need. Even if their plate is full and they have no more time to spare, they still struggle with the idea of saying "no" if they sense someone needs their help. Again, this can be both a good and bad thing. If an empath does not know when to draw the line, they can easily find themselves burned out before they know it. No matter how much they may want to help others, if an empath keeps going with this habit and enforcing no boundaries, soon they will find themselves in a position where they are unable to help anyone. Including themselves.

Survival and Self-Care Tips

Empaths are gentle souls, and it is unfortunate that some people will take advantage of their loving and giving nature. More than anyone else, empaths are in need of survival and self-care tips to protect themselves from being taken advantage of, which can happen a lot if you're unaware. One of the most difficult challenges as an empath can be when people think you're the "strange" one for being so highly sensitive to the world around you. Those who don't have the empathic gift will not be able to comprehend or understand where you're coming from and why you react this way to your surroundings and to the emotions that you pick up from others. People may try to define who you are in an attempt to understand you. Sometimes the words or thoughts they may have about you can be hurtful (even if they don't say it out loud, you're able to sense the way they feel).

Most empaths have at one point, or another experienced an emotional or psychic attack at some point. It can be unbearable when you're not equipped with the safety tips to protect yourself and an immense drain on your energy. What is a psychic attack? Well, it is a discouraging message that is delivered from one individual to another. It often comes from dark thoughts that arise from anger, jealousy, envy, or other negative emotions. Even though empaths are exposed to this on a frequent basis, a lot of empaths who are only just beginning to understand their incredible gift don't know how to cope. It is even harder when the one who is inflicting these emotional and psychic attacks has a strong connection with the empath. They could be family members, friends, or partners and spouses. It's hard enough to balance your emotions without having to deal with the sometimes overbearing emotions of others.

Survival and self-care tips are the ways an empath survives, and if you're struggling to cope with your gift, this is what you can do:

- **Associate With Your Emotions** - The thing about empaths is that they tend to prioritize the emotions and needs of others before themselves. For an empath, it is important to associate with your emotions, understand your feelings, and fulfill your needs.

- **Taking Care of Your Mental and Physical Health** - It is impossible to protect yourself without a healthy mind and body. Get enough rest at night. Exercise for good health. Drink enough water each day. Make healthy food choices. These mantras have been repeated over and over as we scramble for the pursuit of better health. Good health matters because you can do so much more when you're healthy. Think of a time when you have been sick, or when you've injured a certain part of your body, and suddenly, life became a struggle because even the simplest things felt difficult. Do you see how important it is to be healthy? Good health is often taken for granted, and you don't fully learn to appreciate it until you need it most, which is something that needs to change, and that change is going to start with you. Start appreciating how healthy you are right at this moment, and every morning when you wake up, be grateful because you have your health.

- **Meditate Regularly** - Those who avidly do this find that their mind is peaceful and free from worries and mental discomfort, making it easier for them to achieve happiness compared to those who do not practice meditation at all. If you've never tried it, you may not fully understand how sitting quietly for a few minutes every day is going to make a difference in your life, but you would be surprised. By spending a few minutes each day training your mind and making meditation part of your routine, you will discover that your mind gradually is able to find peace a lot easier and finding happiness is something that doesn't seem so elusive anymore, even if you have certain challenges that you may be going through in your life. Even in the most difficult of circumstances, you will find that you're able to remain calm, steady, and still be able to look at the bright side of life. A calmer state of mind means you're in better control of your emotions and you're less likely to feel as overwhelmed.

- **Control Your Energy -** Avoid the circle of people who always give you nothing but negative vibes. That is one way of controlling the energy that you surround yourself with. These energy vampires are only going to drain you if you spend too much time around them. Limiting contact is one way of protecting your emotional and mental state. It is not your duty to continuously try and help those who will not help themselves.

- **Maintain a Positive Living Space -** This can be as simple as keeping your home neat and tidy, a happy sanctuary that you can look forward to coming home to at the end of a long day. Your home should be a place that infuses you with happiness the moment you walk through the door. Try crystals and aromatherapy to infuse your home with positive energy.

- **Practice Shielding Visualization -** This can be a very helpful technique when it comes to protecting yourself from surrounding energies. Fall back on this technique whenever you find yourself in an uncomfortable situation, like when you're in a crowded room, or you're in the presence of an energy vampire. Shielding visualization means you're trying to picture something else in your mind rather than focusing on yourself or any negative energy you might be picking up on. In a way, it is a distraction technique. Take a few deep, measured breathes, focus on your breathing, and then visualize an invisible shield around yourself that is protecting you from negative energy. This protective visualization technique gives your mind something to focus on other than the unwanted energy you might be at risk of absorbing.

- **Don't Be Afraid to Seek Help When You Need It** - Even empaths need someone to talk to and listen to them. Even the strongest people need a shoulder to cry on or someone to turn to when it all feels like too much. If the self-care and survival tips above don't work for you, there is no shame in seeking professional help when you need it. Professional help can be in the form of spiritual guidance, a guardian angel, family member, friend, or partner who genuinely cares for you and is someone you can count on. Professional help can also come in the form of counselors or therapists if you feel like these might work better for you. Seek out professional guidance anytime you feel like you need it because your mental health and wellbeing deserves it.

- **Keep Your Eyes Open** - Keep your eyes open and stay alert to the possibility of toxic personalities in your midst. As soon as you sense them, try to avoid them at all costs before they've had a chance to inflict their damage on you. This preventative action is crucial to preserving your mental and physical state.

- **Define Your Relationship Needs** - Remember how important it is to prioritize your needs? It cannot be stressed enough how vital it is that you learn to take care of yourself. You cannot hope to help others if you're not performing at your very best. Only when you understand what your needs and priorities are will you then be able to create a form of self-protection for yourself, especially when it comes to what you want from the relationships that you have. Each time you feel like you might be in danger of drowning, focus on what your priorities are, define them, and express them. Whenever you don't feel right, don't be afraid to raise the issue and speak up.

How to Thrive Without Feeling Overwhelmed

While being an empath is a wonderful thing, you need to be careful not to experience empathy overload. If you keep absorbing the stress or pain or others continuously, you're going to get over-whelmed in no time at all. Being overwhelmed, of course, makes it very difficult to thrive when you can't focus or think straight.

Emotions have a way of sweeping you up and engulfing you, over-powering you until you feel like you're drowning.

Meditation is one way of calming the mind and protecting your sanity against the unending slew of emotions. Learning to control our minds is one of the most difficult things we can do. It's easy to let our thoughts get the best of us, which is why it is so easy to be consumed by negativity, and external circumstances can affect us to such an extent. The thing about this is, we don't even realize just how severely we are affected by it all because we're not really thinking too much about it. Fluctuations in our moods seem like a normal, everyday occurrence and we brush it off as being part of life and we can't control it. But that's where you're mistaken because you absolutely can do something about it. Meditation is one way of creating that inner space and clarity in your mind that will enable you to always be in firm control of your thoughts despite the circumstances you may be facing. Meditation is how you find that mental balance, so you're never at one extreme or the other. It's always about finding the right balance. You've always been told you need to live a balanced life, eat balanced meals, why not have a balanced mind too? Meditation is a way of bringing you mental clarity, and to change the way you look at the world around you. It is one of the best ways to bring about a sense of fullness and completion, and believe it or not; it is the only way to truly achieve tranquility that is easily accessible to everyone on this planet. True, there may be other temporary forms of serenity, but nothing will come close to bringing you the long-term peace that you seek no matter what you may be going through in your life the way meditation will.

Are there other measures that can be taken so you can thrive instead of feeling overwhelmed by your gift? Absolutely.

- **Set Energy Boundaries** - Healthy boundaries are your ultimate protection against absorbing too many emotions, especially when it comes to fending off toxic personalities. If a person does not respect your boundaries, they are generally toxic, and it is best to steer clear of them. These toxic individuals make it very difficult to have a normal, healthy and respectful relationship with anyone in their life because they will literally just push all your boundaries and they do not know when to stop. Avoid forming relationships with them because it is not worth it in any context. You must start setting up boundaries and be firm about it. Protecting yourself and your own self-worth comes first, and you should never allow yourself to be emotionally bullied by a toxic person, no matter who they are. Do not let someone else make you feel that you are unworthy or inferior; this kind of behavior pattern is dangerous. Setting boundaries helps to protect yourself from them because it helps to limit how much influence they will have over your life. Setting boundaries can be in the form of limiting your time with them or finding a support system to help you manage your emotions after each encounter. It would depend on the situation you may be in. By defining your boundaries, you will come to understand what your limits are when it comes to absorbing surrounding energies too.

- **Be Selfishly Protective of Your Time** - Even empaths deserve some alone time to recuperate from helping, listening, and absorbing the emotions of everyone else. To avoid being overwhelmed, you must be selfishly protective of your time or toxic people, and energy vampires will always have more control over you than they should. If the relationship cannot be fixed, then you need to focus on what can be changed, which is you and the time that you give them. Spend more time with people who bring out the best in you instead, and where possible avoid the toxic person as best that you can. You are not obligated to spend more time with the toxic person than you should, so don't feel guilty about making excuses not to be around them. For the sake of your emotional wellbeing, this is something that must be done.

- **Be Disciplined with Your Quiet Time** - Your quiet time is not something you should willingly compromise on. This is part of your healing process and a way to balance your mental and physical wellbeing. Retreating to your quiet time is the easiest way to keep yourself from feeling emotionally exhausted, and quiet time can be done anywhere, and whenever you feel it. Go for a walk, stretch your muscles, spend time alone until you feel better, taking short breaks throughout the day to step away from people. Your quiet time routine can be anything that works for you.

- **Stay Preoccupied with Your Hobbies** - Everyone has got

things they love to do that brings out their skills and creativity. Playing an instrument, a sport, an activity you like to do, crafts that you like to indulge in to keep your hands and your mind busy, reading a good book in a quiet room by yourself, a hobby is something we all enjoy spending our time on. For an empath, it is important to indulge in these hobbies regularly since they tend to get stressed out very easily.

- **Take A Break from Social Media** - Or media in general, for that matter. Unplugging from the media is essential to avoid overwhelming your empathic senses. Media and social media can be full of negativity, shock value, sensationalism, and extremely traumatic or emotional moments. None of which are good if they're overloading your senses. It doesn't help that we all have minds that are biased toward being attracted to the negative in the first place, even for empaths. Continuously feeding your mind with this type of content is only going to make it harder for you to find peace and balance, so avoid it whenever you can and choose to spend some quiet time alone instead. This is an outstanding self-care and survival practice that is going to help you thrive without feeling overwhelmed.

- **Spend Time in Nature** - Most empaths feel refreshed when they're around nature. If you haven't spend a lot of time in nature lately, it might be time to revisit that again. Whenever you feel overwhelmed, choose to retreat to nature. Go to the beach and listen to the sound of the waves crashing against the shore. Go for a walk in the park and listen to the birds singing. Feel the breeze caress your skin and take in a deep breath as you lose yourself in your surroundings. Spend as much time in nature as you need until you feel refreshed again.

- **Don't Make Other People's Problems Your Own -** This is only going to make you feel pressured to help, even when you can't. Not everyone's problems can be fixed, and it is important not to take on their burden and make it your own. Help them as best you can, but don't make the problem a personal one. Your passion for wanting to help is one of your best qualities as an empath, but the truth is you simply cannot fix the world on your own. You need to know when to step back and say this is something you cannot help with.

CONCLUSION

Thank you for making it through to the end of *Empath by Rhonda Swan*, let's hope it was informative and able to provide you with all of the tools you need to achieve your goals whatever they may be.

Being an empath is wonderful. Not everyone has the ability to listen to another with their entire body, mind, and soul. Not everyone has the power to heal others and help them through their pain quite like the way an empath can. If you don't know you're an empath, it's easy to feel like there's something wrong with you. It's easy to struggle to comprehend why you feel so emotional and so sensitive. It's easy to believe when people tell you that you're over-reacting or you're too sensitive about something.

Being an empath is not without its challenges, but these can be managed when you know what you're dealing with. The important thing to remember is not to neglect yourself. Take care of your mind, body, and spirit because you need as much healing as everyone else does. If you need to take some time being on your own, recharging and replenishing your energy reserves, do it and don't feel guilty about it. Your ability to help others becomes diminished when you feel like you are burned out and running on empty yourself. Feeling discouraged, frustrated, upset, and really sad, and sometimes you can't explain why, then learn to take a step back and focus your energy on yourself. You can't help someone else if you are in need of healing too. You need to take that time to figure out what your emotions are and how to separate that from the emotions of others. Hopefully, now that you understand a little more about what it means to be an empath, you'll be able to better regulate your emotions and minimize the moments when you feel so overwhelmed by your gift.

Finally, if you found this book useful in any way, a review on Amazon is always appreciated!